YOU CAN PRAY WITH POWER

LLOYD JOHN OGILVIE

GL
Regal Books
A Division of GL Publications
Ventura, California, U.S.A.

Published by Regal Books
A Division of GL Publications
Ventura, California 93006
Printed in U.S.A.

Library of Congress Cataloging-in-Publication data applied for.

1 2 3 4 5 6 7 8 9 10 / 92 91 90 89 88

Rights for publishing this book in other languages are contracted by Gospel Literature International (GLINT) foundation. GLINT also provides technical help for the adaptation, translation, and publishing of Bible study resources and books in scores of languages worldwide. For further information, contact GLINT, Post Office Box 488, Rosemead, California, 91770, U.S.A., or the publisher.

YOU CAN
PRAY
WITH
POWER

CONTENTS

INTRODUCTION

Every week I receive hundreds of letters containing questions and expressions of urgent need from my congregation and my church's national television ministry. The deepest need expressed in dozens of ways is to learn how to pray with power.

I have kept a record of what people ask about prayer. These provided me the basis of a prolonged study of the Scriptures on the theme of prayer. The result was not only an opportunity to respond personally from the Bible to each letter, but to do a series of messages on the television program in direct response to the questions people raised. The fresh insight the Lord revealed to me about the power of prayer is the thrust of this book.

What breathing is to our physical life, prayer is to our spiritual life. It is the very essence of the abundant life. Why then do we find so much difficulty in praying? Why do we have so many questions about how to pray effectively?

I am convinced that it is because of a profound misunderstanding of prayer, who initiates it, and what should happen to us when we pray. The purpose of this book is to expose what God meant prayer to be and what He has said about the secret of dynamic conversation with Him when we pray.

Prayer is more than saying our prayers. It is communion with the Lord who wants to give us His mind, guidance, and power. Most of all, He wants to give us the gift of Himself. He calls us into prayer to impart that awesome gift.

There is a central theme that runs all through this book. It is that prayer starts with God. He is the initiator, instigator, and inspiration of prayer. I try to weave that exciting conviction through all the chapters which deal with the deepest needs and urgent questions which people constantly ask about prayer. With the essential secret of prayer as God's idea, I deal with how to talk with Him, how to make all of life a prayer, how prayer transforms us, how to pray for people, and what to do when our prayers seem to be unanswered. Then I press on to deal with how prayer enables healing, why we pray in Jesus' name, and how God can guide our decisions. The final chapter offers the much needed gift of endurance when life brings us to the end of our resources and we're tempted to give up.

The whole book is meant to be a dialogue between friends who long to discover how to pray with power. Everywhere I go, I talk to people who are struggling to find power to live life more fully—to discover how to realize their full potential. Here's my formula worked out over the years of studying the Scriptures and the great prayer warriors of the ages.

I am thankful for the fact that these chapters have been written in conversation with a congregation seeking to discover all that the Lord offers through prayer. Each chapter was preached and then revised in the light of insights and comments by my friends in my congregation and the television audience. These front line troops of the Lord were the focus of my efforts to explore the deeper mysteries of prayer power. The result is a book that has been tested and tried by real people who echo Jesus' disciples' plea, "Lord, teach us to pray!" That was also my urgent quest as I wrote this book—to put into your hands as my readers, the practical and applicable insights the Lord gave me and deepened in conversation with real people like you who seek to pray with power.

My special thanks to Jeri Gonzalez, my administrative assistant, for her typing of the manuscript and for her enthusiasm for this project.

Now I want to open my heart and mind to you and pour out the exciting, fresh vision the Lord has given me for you about adventuresome prayer.

Lloyd John Ogilvie

CHAPTER ONE
PRAYER STARTS WITH GOD

I want to share a revolutionary thought. It has changed my life. My whole perception of prayer has been transformed by it. As a result, my prayers and praying have become more exciting than ever.

I've been a Christian for thirty-five years. Far too many of those years were spent with a totally incorrect conception of prayer. I labored with the misapprehension that prayer was my idea, that conversation with God was initiated by me. That idea took on the heavy baggage of believing that I had to get God's attention and that He would listen and respond if I said the right words and led a life worthy of His condescension. Prayer became burdensome, laborious. Often I was reluctant to pray when I needed to the most because of things I'd done or said which made me feel ashamed or embarrassed by a less than perfect life. The conception that prayer was initiated by me left it up to my moods and spiritual readiness.

Then one day a few years ago, I happened on a combination of Scriptures from the Old and New Testaments which exploded the tight, constricted, and limited view of prayer I had held. They all thundered forth a truth which I desperately needed to learn and live.

Stated simply it is this: prayer starts with God. It is His idea. The desire to pray is the result of God's greater desire to talk with us. He has something to say when we feel the urge to pray. He is the initiator. The keen desire to begin and end the day with prolonged prayer is His gift. The sense of need to pray for challenges or opportunities throughout the day is because He has wisdom and insight He wants to impart. When we face crises and suddenly feel the urge to pray for strength, that feeling is a response to the Lord's invasion of our minds which triggers the thought of needing help which is congealed into the desire to pray. He, not us, was the author of the longing for His help.

I want to share these Scriptures with you which have caused this renaissance in my prayers. The message they convey tells us something magnificent about God and the wondrous way He has created us for communion and conversation with Him. He is the instigator, implementor, and inspiration of prayer.

The Answer Is Prepared Before We Pray

The first is Isaiah 65:24. Listen to what the Lord Himself tells us about prayer. "It shall come to pass that before they call, I will answer; and while they are still speaking, I will hear." That tells us that the answer to our prayers is prepared before we pray. The desire to talk to the Lord about our needs comes from Him. Prayer begins in the mind of God, invades our minds, is formulated into a clarification of what He wants to do or give, and then is articulated in our words. He is more ready to hear than we are to pray!

This propitious promise of the Lord was made in response to an excruciating question asked by Israel, recorded in Isaiah 64:12. The people had sinned and felt the judgment of God. They were distant from Him; He had never left His people. Their sorrow had reached its height when they cried out, "Wilt thou keep silent . . . ?" *(RSV)*. The response of grace was mediated through the prophet. There will come a time when not only will the Lord answer, but His answer will precede the petition, and prayer will be the response of God's call rather than just His response to our call. This prophetic revelation of the nature of prayer is in anticipation of the messianic age when God Himself would come to reconcile and redeem His people. The people to whom Isaiah wrote never fully appreciated the wondrous offer God made in this statement. It was only after the incarnation and Pentecost that a new creation was prepared to appropriate it. It was not until the liberation of the bondage of the will took place on Calvary and the new creatures in Christ were filled with His Spirit at Pentecost that a new Israel, the Church, was born and could accept and utilize the awesome promise the Lord had made so long before.

Thomas Carlyle once said, "Prayer is and remains a native and deep impulse of the soul of man." That sounds lovely, but I don't believe it. No one naturally desires to pray. Our volitional capacity is debilitated until we are loved, liberated, and regenerated by Christ. It is after we have been transformed by the cross and filled with the Spirit that we can experience the enlivening of the "native and deep impulse" to pray. And even after we've been born again, it is the Lord who motivates us to pray. It is part of His prevenient, beforehand grace. Not even the longing for God is our accomplishment. It is birthed in our souls by the Lord who created us for communion with Him.

Commenting on this promise in Isaiah, Luther said, "Our prayer pleases God because He has commanded it, made promises, and given form to our prayer. For that reason, He is pleased with our prayer, He requires it and delights in it, because He promises, commands, and shapes it . . . . Then He says, 'I will hear.' It is not only guaranteed, but it is actually already obtained."[1]

He Is the Implementor of Prayer

At the same time I was pondering the implications of the Lord's offer in Isaiah, He led me to rediscover another passage which deepened my understanding of that promise. I read 1 John 5:12-15 with new eyes in my heart. The Lord comes to us as the implementor of prayer. The Apostle John asserted the secret of dynamic praying in the context of our life in Christ. "He who has the Son has life; he who does not have the Son of God does not have life" (v. 12). The apostle wanted his readers in the early Church to be sure of their relationship, now and forever, in Christ. He went on to state the reason why he had written was: "that you may know that you have eternal life, and that you may continue to believe in the name of the Son of God" (v. 13). For John, the Son was *Immanuel,* God with us, and continuing with us to guide us. His Christian life was not an anxious searching for the Lord but moment by moment response to His impinging, invading imminence. Then in verses 14 and 15, John sounds the same joyous note we heard in the Isaiah promise. "Now this is the confidence that we have in Him, that if we ask anything according to His will, He hears us. And if we know that He hears us, whatever we ask, we know that we have the petitions that we have asked of Him."

I quickly checked the Greek text to review words I had studied so often before. Now they came alive in new vitality and freshness. The words for "confidence" and "in Him" leaped off the page. Confidence is *perresia* in the

In prayer, He makes known to us what is His will so that we can ask for what He longs to give. He calls us into His presence because He has the answer to our needs nad questions.

Greek. The word means boldness. It is a compound word made up of *pan*—all, and *ressia*—to tell, meaning freedom to speak boldly. Prayer is freedom to speak freely and boldly to the Lord who has instigated our prayer. But then I discovered again that the English translation of the next words do not catch the exciting implication of the original Greek. The confidence we have in prayer is what "we have in Him." *Pros auton* really means "toward Him" or "face-to-face" with Him. *Pros* is from *prosōpton*, "face." Prayer, for John, was face-to-face communication with Christ as a part of the eternal quality of life we have in Him which gives us boldness. Face to face, first we listen to Him intently and then we can speak with intrepidity.

And who starts the face-to-face conversation? The Lord! John makes that clear in 4:19, "We love Him because He first loved us." He is the prime mover in salvation, the gift of faith, and the initiation of prayer. In prayer, He makes known to us what is His will so that we can ask for what He longs to give. He calls us into His presence because He has the answer to our needs and questions. "If we ask anything according to His will, He hears us." Our assurance that He hears us is that He is the one who asked for the conversation. He would not call us to prayer and then refuse to listen or be inattentive to our prayer. That's the confidence, boldness, we have: prayer is our response to His call. In the time of face-to-face communion He makes clear what it is that we are to ask for in the needs He has come to us to help us solve.

So when we do ask, it is with the confidence that we are asking for what He is prepared to release for us. "And if we know that He hears us, whatever we ask, we know that we have the petitions that we have asked of Him." We know before we ask, because the content of our asking has been guided by Him. The same assurance had been stated by John earlier in his epistle. "And by this we know that we are of the truth, and shall assure our hearts before Him. For if our heart condemns us, God is greater than our heart, and knows all things. Beloved, if our heart does not condemn us, we have confidence toward God. And whatever we ask we receive from Him, because we keep His commandments and do those things that are pleasing in His sight. And this is His commandment: that we should believe on the name of His Son Jesus Christ and love one another, as He gave us commandment" (1 John 3:19-23). The basics of prayer have been given already in the commandment. The Lord reminds us of this as He calls us into prayer and then as the instigative agent of prayer, spells out the specific details of the commandment to believe and love in particular situations.

Allow me to illustrate. Recently one of my friends was in trouble. He needed my help, and yet was not sure I had time to help. So I asked one of my sons to talk to the man and offer my help. My son said to him, "My dad really wants to help and he's willing to do the following things." He enumerated the personal and practical assistance I wanted to give. The intervention of someone as close to me as my son convinced the man of my real heart in the matter. When the man came to me with the request he did not have to wonder about my readiness to help. He came with the confidence of inside information of what I was willing to do. When he asked me to do exactly what I'd offered through my son, I did it immediately.

Or consider the world of negotiation in business. A man in my congregation confided that settling a difficult matter is so much easier when he knows what the other person is willing to do. If he can get someone to intercede for him to find out what the other party's terms are, he can make an offer which he knows will be accepted. On the other hand, when he wants someone to bid at a price he is willing to accept, he gets an emissary to go to the person to disclose his willingness to sell and the price he's open to accept. When the offer comes, he responds because it complies with his terms.

Some years ago, I needed a grant from a large foundation for a strategic program in my church. A trusted friend interceded for me. He talked to the head of the foundation and arranged for an interview for me. The man liked the idea and suggested how I should draft the proposal to be sure it was met with enthusiasm and approval by the board of directors in charge of the foundation. When I followed his suggestions, the proposal was accepted by the foundation and the grant was made. All the guesswork was taken out of my application. The board was responsible for distribution of funds provided by a great benefactor in America. It had to distribute the funds; all I had to do was prepare something which was within the qualifications of the policies of the board. I could not have known that without the help of the head of the board who helped me ask in a way I could be confident would be accepted.

These illustrations touch only the fringes of the central truth John is seeking to communicate. Christ is the heart of God with us. He guides us in what and how to ask. When we ask in keeping with what He has revealed to us, we ask with the boldness that the answer is on the way. "We know that we have the petitions that we have asked of Him." The word "know," *oidamen*, is used twice: If we know that He hears us, then we know that we have what He has guided us to ask. A.T. Robertson says that the Greek implies "the confidence of possession by anticipation."[2] The Lord gives us boldness to say what He has told us to pray!

Inspiration Comes from Him

The third passage of Scripture which confirmed for me this truth that prayer starts with God is Romans 8:26-30. This particular passage affirms that the inspiration for praying comes from Him. Again the Spirit of the Lord, the present Christ, is the initiator of the desire, content, and assurance of prayer. Note how Paul developed the same sublime theme. "Likewise the Spirit also helps in our weaknesses. For we do not know what we should pray for as we ought, but the Spirit Himself makes intercession for us with groanings which cannot be uttered. Now He who searches the hearts knows what the mind of the Spirit is, because He makes intercession for the saints according to the will of God. And we know that all things work together for good to those who love God, to those who are the called according to His purpose. For whom He foreknew, He also predestined to be conformed to the image of His Son, that He might be the firstborn among many brethren. Moreover whom He predestined, these He also called; whom He called, these He also justified; and whom He justified, these He also glorified."

The full impact of this is realized by starting at the end. We are called and appointed to belong to the Lord. That election and call was according to His predestined plan. We did not choose; we were chosen. That's where it all began. The Lord singled us out to belong to Him. As His children, He wants us to accept His love lavishly given on the cross and offered in His own presence in His Spirit. He wants to make us like Himself. That requires the quality of face-to-face communion which is prayer. His desire is for all things in our lives to work together to accomplish the plan He has for each of us. That plan is His will for us. The word *the-lēma* is used in Greek for "will" in this passage. It means

His purpose is to bring our desires into alignment with His desires so we can ask for that which will be part of all things working together for good.

desire. The Lord has a desire for all of us, a purpose for us to accomplish. But He does not leave us, after we are born again, with no training or help in accomplishing this purpose of being conformed into His own image. He invades our subconscious with preconscious longings and urgings which are manifested in the conscious desire to pray, seeking His desires for us. The Father, the Son, and the Holy Spirit are one. The Spirit is the reigning glorified Christ with us. This is what Paul made undeniably clear to the Galatians. "And because you are sons, God has sent forth the Spirit of His Son into your hearts, crying out, 'Abba, Father!' " (Gal. 4:6). The Spirit of the Son comes to us in our weaknesses. He calls us to prayer and then gives us the "groanings which cannot be uttered." What does this mean? My understanding is that the groanings are the preconscious longings which He eventually articulates through us in helping us to put into words what He wants us to pray. It is not that the intercession is done for us, for that would deny the cooperation with the Lord for which we were created. At first the invasion of the Spirit produces the longing to pray. Then when we feel the need to pray, but still don't know how or what to pray, He provides that also. Because He knows our hearts and is the heart of the Lord, He brings them into congruity. His purpose is to bring our desires into alignment with His desires so we can ask for that which will be part of all things working together for good.

Recently I had a misunderstanding with a cherished friend which resulted in a broken relationship. The startling thing was that for a time I didn't want to find a reconciliation. I chalked it up to irreconcilable differences which precluded the possibility of forgiveness and a new beginning. I was hurt and angry. My plan was to forget the whole mess. Some weeks later, an uneasiness began to grow in me. I couldn't shake the man out of my mind. That was followed by a mysterious desire to pray about him. When I responded to the inner urgings to pray, I noticed a difference in my attitude. As I prayed, I was given new empathy for what might have caused the man's behavior. I was given a completely different picture of the needs inside him; and then I asked for a way to communicate acceptance and forgiveness. As I lingered in prayer, a strategy was unfolded for what I needed to do and say. I had the deep conviction that the plan came from the Lord. Therefore when I asked for His help to accomplish His will in the matter, I could ask with boldness. The inner disquiet, like an inaudible wordless groaning, turned into clarity and was articulated in a request for strength to do what the Lord had promised He would do through me if I were willing. A new, ready will worked with my imagination to form the picture of how it would be accomplished. And that's exactly the way it turned out. The Lord was initiator and inspiration from start to finish.

The same process occurred in a tough decision I had to make recently. I thought I knew what the Lord wanted and did not pray a lot about it. When the decision was made, I had no peace. There was a jangling static in my spirit. It lasted for days. When sleep was interrupted by the disturbance, I knew something was very wrong. I asked the Lord to be very clear. I asked Him how to pray. A specific request was given me to make. If the disturbance was from Him I asked that it continue and grow. If the decision I had made was right and the disquiet was simply my own fear of implementing it, I was led to ask that the disturbance be taken away. You guessed it: the static grew to unbearably high decibles. That led me to confess, "Lord, now I know I'm on the wrong track. Show me what you want me to do." After hours of quiet listening, I reversed the hastily made decision. As I prayed, a new direction formed in my mind, pictured by my imagination. When I decided to follow the new direction, the jangling static inside subsided. An inner calm and confidence grew in its place. Then with holy boldness, I asked for what the Spirit had formed in my mind. When I asked I knew that I was assured of the answer. Subsequently, the decision was worked out by the Spirit's power exactly as He detailed it in prayer. Again, He had been the source of the disturbance, the desire to review the previous decision, the architect of the new plan, the communicator of the different direction, and the instigator of a boldness to ask for what He had imparted.

All these passages I have shared with you are the basis of everything else I want to say about prayer. Hold that basic thought. It will be woven through all that we will discuss together. *Prayer starts with God.* Our desire to pray is the result of His call to prayer. He has something to say. Our responsibility is to listen to what He wants to give us for our problems and potentials. He will make it clear. Then we can say with boldness:

I sought the Lord, and afterward I knew
   He moved my soul to seek Him, seeking me;
It was not I that found, O Savior true,
   No, I was found of Thee.[3]

Notes

1. Hilton Oswald, *Luther's Works, Isaiah* (Saint Louis: Concordia Publishing House, 1975), vol. 17, p. 393.
2. A.T. Robertson, *Word Pictures in the New Testament* (Nashville: Broadman Press, 1930), vol 6, p. 243.
3. Author unknown.

For Further Thought . . .

1. How do we know that our prayers are answered before we even pray? Review Isaiah 65:24.

2. "The Lord gave us boldness to say what He has told us to pray," says Dr. Ogilvie. What does this statement mean to you?

3. The author cites 3 passages of Scripture that confirm the truth that prayer starts with God. Name these passages and memorize at least one.

4. Name specific times you have prayed for a person or situation and then watched the answer unfold in the very way in which the Holy Spirit guided you to pray.

CHAPTER TWO

EIGHT STEPS TO EFFECTIVE PRAYER

Successful prayer is not measured by how much we get from God, but how much of Him gets into us and our daily circumstances and relationships. Prayer is not a "gimme game" but a grace gift. It is not being able to convince God of what we ought to have, but allowing Him to convince us of what we need and He is ready to give.

That's the magnificent truth Jesus taught His disciples when they came to Him with the request, "Lord, teach us to pray" (Luke 11:1). His response was to give them an example of prayer in what we have called the Lord's Prayer. In it we discover the steps of effective prayer. And then to drive home the context in which these steps were to be realized, the Lord gave several parables which stressed God's availability, His readiness to hear and respond, and His desire to give us Himself.

He startles us with the parable of the importune friend who goes to a neighbor seeking bread at midnight and is refused at first and then, because of his persistence, is granted his request. No such importunity is necessary with God. Jesus says, "And I say to you, ask, and it will be given you; seek, and you will find; knock, and it will be opened to you. For every one who asks receives, and he

who seeks finds, and to him who knocks it will be opened"
(Luke 11:9-10). The gracious generosity of God is established as the ambience in which we pray.

If that startles us, the second parable shocks us. "If a
son asks for bread from any father among you, will he give
him a stone? Or if he asks for a fish, will he give him a ser-
pent instead of a fish? Or if he asks for an egg, will he offer
him a scorpion?" (vv. 11-12). We feel a tug on our filial
hearts. What parent would do that? Jesus has our attention, indeed! We are ready to hear His "how much more"
comparison of God to earthly parents. "If you then, being
evil, know how to give good gifts to your children, how
much more will your heavenly Father give the Holy Spirit
to those who ask Him!" (v. 13). What Jesus is saying to us
is that the purpose, power and progression of prayer is a
gift of the Holy Spirit. When we ask how to pray, God
gives Himself. He gives us the motive and power to pray.
He instructs us in the progression of our conversation with
Him. In a vivid way Jesus is predicting His own return in
the presence of the Holy Spirit to guide us in our prayers.
He creates the longing to pray, helps us to know what to
say, and then guides us each step of the way. Prayer is to
expand our hearts until they are capable not just of saying
our prayers, but of receiving the Lord Himself.

In the power of the Spirit, the Lord comes to us and
says, "Behold, I stand at the door and knock. If anyone
hears My voice and opens the door, I will come in to him
and dine with him, and he with Me" (Rev. 3:20). As the
honored guest of our hearts He shows us how to pray. He
created us and knows how crucial it is that our capacity of
desire be directed creatively. Emerson said, "Prayer is the
soul's sincere desire." Desire marshals our energies and
prioritizes what we think is important. That's why the
Lord wants to shape our desires as He guides our prayers.

Prayer is not getting the Lord's attention, but allowing Him to lead us in praying for what He is more ready to give than we may be to ask.

We are desiring all the time and, therefore, are really praying all the time. We need prolonged times with the Lord so that we can experience the reorientation of our desires around His desires for us.

Robert Murry M'Cheyne said something which has radically changed my conception of how this works. He said, "If I could hear Christ praying for me in the next room, I would not fear a million enemies. Yet distance makes no difference. He is praying for me." Profound prayer is listening in on our Lord's prayers for us and then praying after Him what He has modeled for us to pray. Prayer is not getting the Lord's attention, but allowing Him to lead us in praying for what He is more ready to give than we may be to ask.

The essence of this quality of prayer was expressed by a son who tenderly said to his dad, "I really appreciate all you've done for me, but my deepest desire is just to be with you. . . . I want to become like you, Dad." That's the dominant desire the Lord creates within us for our prayers. And then we are ready to hear from Him how to pray. In my experience, He leads us through the following eight steps of effective conversation.

Adoration

All great praying begins with adoration. God does not need our praise as much as we need to give it. Praise is like a thermostat that opens the heart to flow in communion with God. Hallowing God's name is enumerating His attributes. When we think magnificently about God's nature we become open to experience afresh His glory in our lives. I once took a course in creative conversation. The key thing I rediscovered was that there can be no deep exchange with another person until we have established the value of that person to us. Just as profound con-

versation with another person results from our communicating that person's worth to us, so too, we become
receptive to what God wants to do in our lives when we
have taken time to tell Him what He means to us. Don't
hurry through adoration. Everything else depends on it.
Tell God what He means to you, pour out your heart in
unhurried moments of exultation. Allow Him to remind
you of aspects of His nature you need to claim in the subsequent steps of prayer. Don't forget He is the leader of
the conversation. The more we praise the Lord, the more
we will be able to think His thoughts after Him throughout
our prayer. He loosens the tissues of our brains to become
channels of His Spirit.

Praise is the ultimate level of relinquishment. When
we praise God for not only all He is but what He is doing in
our lives, we reach a liberating stage of surrender. Often
when we begin our prayers, we don't feel like adoration.
Sometimes we wonder what God is doing with us in the
difficulties and trials of life. Praising Him reestablishes the
fact in our minds that He knows what He is doing and
makes us receptive to His guidance in those very needs.

I've experienced that repeatedly. When I'm inundated
with problems, my temptation is to rush past adoration to
tell the Lord the particular thing I think He ought to do to
help me. It never works. When I take time to reflect on
the greatness of God in spite of my circumstances, I am
much more ready to receive fresh wisdom when I pray
about specifics.

A good way to recapture the power of praise is to read
the Psalms. I find a creative two-week adoration assurance is to read Psalms 95 through 108, one each day as a
prelude to my own praise. They reestablish my trust in
God's power, providence, and all-knowing love. My heart
begins to sing again and then soar in communion with the

Lord. The point is that God wants us to enjoy Him! He delights to bless us when we let go of our worries and fears in unfettered praise.

There are times when I've found it helpful to begin my prayers by saying, "I love you, Lord. Let me tell you why." Then I rehearse in my mind all that He's been for me. Soon He takes over and leads me in remembering His goodness and grace. In times of difficulty, dark moods are lifted, troubled spirits are transformed, and an unwilling heart is made receptive. Or in bright times of success and smooth sailing, my happiness is maximized into pure joy. But whatever the circumstances of life, adoration creates the sublime delight of being in the presence of the Lord. Worship in the ancient English means "worth-shape," or establishing the worth, the wonder, and the glory of God in our minds and hearts. Adoration is the beginning of powerful praying. God created us to receive and return His love.

Contrition

The heights of our adoration prepares us for the depths of our confession. *The second step of prayer is contrition.* Once we have beheld the holiness of God, we become aware of our need to talk to Him about anything we've done or said that has denied His plan and purpose for us. But here again, the secret of confession is to allow the Lord to guide us. We think of confession as our act of setting things right with God. Not so! In Hebrew, confession means to show, point out, or acknowledge. In Greek the word is *homologeō*, "to say the same after." Authentic confession is to allow the Lord to press to the deeper levels of our lives to point out what He wants us to confess. So often we rehearse the surface failures. He digs deeper into the motive of our rebellious hearts. Often things which we decided to hide or equivocate become the focus of His all-knowing eye. Confession is to say, "Lord, show me anything which you see that is standing between you and me or between me and any other human being which needs to be confessed, or said after you." Sin means to miss the mark. What we consider our sins may be far less serious than what the Lord wants to cleanse from us. It is an awesome experience to allow the Lord to show us ourselves. We cannot take the shock apart from His love which will not let us go.

> Search all my sense, and know my heart
>   Who only can make known
> And let the deep, the hidden part
>   To me be fully shown.[1]

We cannot pray like that anywhere but at the foot of the cross. We can confess what God tells us to say after Him when we are sure we are forgiven even before we acknowledge the deeper sin beneath our more obvious sins. What is involved in true confession is to surrender the management of our lives to the Lord. He wants to make us new creatures. He knows what needs to be changed, amended, or corrected.

I am constantly amazed at how this happens. Recently, I felt a twinge of jealousy because of an opportunity given to a friend of mine. The next day I spread out the whole situation to the Lord. Much to my astonishment, He dug down into the roots of the sin. The longer I lingered in the confession portion of my prayers that day, the more I realized that I had drifted into a lack of appreciation for the tremendous opportunities the Lord had lavished on me. That changed jealousy into praise for the unique, different ways the Lord had decided to use me and my friend. The feeling was gone and has not returned.

This personal illustration is duplicated in the lives of people with whom I counsel. So often they come to me with the need to confess some sin which is unsettling them. I've learned from experience to help people ask the Lord to show them the deeper cause and motivation. Then prayer therapy with them in which we are silent after asking the Lord to probe deeper, usually exposes the raw nerve which really needs His healing forgiveness. The Lord is up to a great thing in transforming us and He wants nothing in His way. "Would not God search this out? For He knows the secrets of the heart" (Ps. 44:21). It is a source of comfort that He knows all about us. Peace comes when we say after Him what He knows and experience unlimited grace in spite of anything we've done or been.

Thanksgiving

And how shall we respond to a love like that? We are ready for the *next step which flows naturally—thanksgiving*. Thanksgiving is not just listing our blessings, but acknowledging the greatest blessing of all—the unmerited grace of the cross. It is from this side of Calvary and the open tomb of Easter that we can repeat Psalm 106, verse 1. "Praise the Lord! Oh, give thanks to the Lord, for He is good! For His mercy endures forever." The cross revealed the forgiving heart of God; the resurrection was His vindication and validation of Christ's atonement for our sins. How can we ever thank Him enough?

Here again the Spirit of the Lord leads us just as He did in adoration and confession. He brings to our remembrance all that He has done for us. We are all tempted to take the Lord's blessings for granted. We forget to say thanks. He knows that the attitude of gratitude is the key

to greatness. The more we thank God for who He is and
what He does for us the more He is able to bless us further.

Commitment

I have discovered that thanksgiving prepares me to
commit all my problems and needs to the Lord. A survey
of the past goodness of the Lord leads me to a confidence
of trusting my relationships and responsibilities to Him.
Commitment is the fourth step of effective prayer. On the
cross, Jesus repeated a prayer which every Hebrew child
learned at his mother's knee. "Into Your hand I commit my
spirit" (Ps. 31:5). It is a good motto for this stage of our
conversation with the Lord. Another is Psalm 37:5, "Commit your way to the Lord, trust also in Him, and He shall
bring it to pass." The same releasing quality is expressed
in Proverbs 16:3, "Commit your works to the Lord, and
your thoughts will be established." All these Scriptures
offer a great promise. Commitment leads to openness. We
can discover the Lord's guidance in these challenges which
have been turned over completely to Him.

I can't stress too much the crucial importance of this
step of prayer. Commitment is the missing ingredient of
contemporary Christianity and the reason so many miss
the power of prayer. Many of us believe in the Lord, but
have never made a commitment of our lives to Him. We
are running our own lives. Prayer becomes a kind of magic
to get God to do what we think is best for our lives. We
break the first commandment: we have another god
before the Lord—ourselves. When a crisis strikes we run
to the Lord for help. It's usually to get His assistance to do
what we've planned.

Too severe an analysis? How do you feel about that
from your own experience of prayer? Ever sought God's

Him or the result of His guidance?

When I talk with people who are experiencing a lack of power in their prayers or seldom sense the presence of the Lord, so often the cause is traced back to the absence of complete commitment. I talked to a man recently who was facing difficulties with his daughter. Her life did not reflect his values or his beliefs. Tension and hostility sparked like electricity whenever they were together. The man prayed about his daughter's problems daily. There was no question in his mind what his daughter should do and be, and he told God repeatedly. When he came to see me about what he called his "impossible problem," I felt led to ask him how he was praying about it. His response clearly indicated the real problem. He had never surrendered the need to the Lord, asking what He wanted him to be as a father and a communicator of affirmation and encouragement to his daughter's efforts to find out who she was and where she was going. He had to become a friend to establish the right to be heard. Imperious commands only caused greater rebellion. When he stopped telling the Lord what to do, and committed the broken relationship between him and his daughter, he began to see the quality of father she needed. He asked the Lord to show him the person he needed to be with her. The result was that he began empathizing instead of criticizing. He not only was able to help her make some crucial decisions about her life, but discovered the secret of dynamic prayer. The only things which can ultimately hurt us and those we love are the things we refuse to commit to the Lord's wise and incisive guidance.

What are the problems and perplexities on your mind right now? In what areas are you clenching your fists and saying, "I've got to take care of this on my own"? Open those fists and put the needs into the trustworthy hands of those fists and put the needs into the trustworthy hands of our Lord. He is worthy of the trust. He's been handling people and problems for thousands of years. He is able. Let go! When you do, you are ready for the adventure of the next step of conversation with the Lord.

Meditation

Commitment is followed by meditation. This is creative listening. When we unfold all our needs before the Lord and listen attentively, He will speak through the Scriptures, our thoughts, and our inner feelings. When we honestly say, "Lord, what do you want me to do?" He answers. The psalmist had that assurance. "The meditation of my heart shall bring understanding" (Ps. 49:3).

Keep meditation at the center of prayer. It is the most decisive aspect of prayer. Everything leads up to it; everything flows from it. From it we learn what to ask in subsequent portions of prayer for others, ourselves, and specific situations. Our theme in this book is emphasized again. God delights to reveal to us what He wants us to pray. Then our prayers are in keeping with what He has prepared to give.

Often I sit or kneel for a long time waiting for guidance on how to pray about particular needs. I would be less than honest if I suggested that an answer on what to pray for comes in the first few times I ask for guidance on how to pray about a situation. Patience is not my character trait. I want action from myself, others, even God, when I want it. But I have learned to give the Lord what I call conditioning time. When I see a need for guidance forming on the horizon of my future, I try to commit it to Him, renew that commitment daily, and be open for His perfectly timed direction. As the time for action or a decision draws near, there is a confluence of Scripture, the devel-

We are given wisdom and insight we could not have achieved by ourselves. The wonder of it all is that the Creator and Sustainer of the universe is able and willing to inspire our thoughts so we know how to pray for what He wills and wants to give.

pray when the time is right. The Lord knew all along what He wanted me to pray—it was I who needed to be prepared to ask according to His will.

In the process of meditation, the most complicated problems yield to solutions. We are given wisdom and insight we could not have achieved by ourselves. The wonder of it all is that the Creator and Sustainer of the universe is able and willing to inspire our thoughts so we know how to pray for what He wills and wants to give.

Intercession and Supplication

I have stressed meditation at length because it transforms *the next two steps of prayer—intercession and supplication*. Without meditation, prayers for others and ourselves will be ineffective and lacking in power.

Prayers for people will be dealt with more completely in a subsequent chapter. At this point I want to stress our calling to be part of the priesthood of all believers. The mystery of the Lord's providential management of the lives of His people is that He often waits to bless the people around us until we pray. Prolonged meditation about the needs of people gives us the content of our prayers of intercession. As priests of the Lord we have authority to go to Him about people and bring His assurance and courage to them. "You are a chosen generation, a royal priesthood" (1 Pet. 2:9). Our calling to be priests armed with the power of intercessory prayer goes back to the strategy of God given to Moses at Mount Sinai. The Lord declared that He wanted all His people to cooperate with Him in accomplishing His purposes through prayer for others.

The secret of how to intercede for others comes from Christ. Hebrews 7:25 shows us the way. "Therefore He is also able to save to the uttermost those who come to God also able to save to the uttermost those who come to God through Him, since He ever lives to make intercession for them." In our prayers for others, our task is to listen in on His intercession. What would He pray for the people on our hearts? He reveals that in our meditation. Then we can pray with both authority and confidence. To pray for another person in Christ's name means by His power, but also through His guidance of what to pray. He gives us that discernment for our priesthood as intercessors. The Lord wants to bind His people together in mutual love and concern through prayer for each other. And the awesome thing is that through our prayers His blessings, power, healing, and guidance are given the people for whom we pray!

Prayer for our own needs is done in the same assurance. It is as if the Lord Jesus comes to us, puts His arms of love around us and says, "Dear friend, you've told me about your concerns, committed them to me and have asked how to pray. Now this is what I want for you." The one who said, "I will never leave you or forsake you" will not leave us confused or without direction for our prayers of supplication. Our Lord is faithful. He has a maximum plan for all of us. He will make it plain. The Lord never contradicts the Ten Commandments, His own message as Jesus of Nazareth, or the implications of His love for each situation. He will not guide us to do anything which will frustrate our union with Him. His ultimate will is that we know, love, and serve Him. He shows us what love demands and guides us in specific steps to take. When we miss His best and confess it to Him, He graciously weaves that into the tapestry of His final goal. We belong to Him, and if we are willing He will make each step of our path clearly lighted by daily, moment-by-moment guidance. We have a wonderful Friend to help us pray with power.

Dedication

Finally, He leads us into the last step of effective praying. He says, "Will you dare to implement your part in what I have guided you to pray?" Our actions either confirm or contradict what He has led us to pray. *Dedication is the action step of powerful prayer.* So often our prayers clarify what love demands in specific action. Our capacity to receive further intimacy with Him in prayer is dependent on implementing anything He clarifies we must do in faithfulness and obedience to Him. So often each step of prayer we've talked about leads to the necessity of following orders. Jesus put a great emphasis on the balance between hearing and doing. He closed the Sermon on the Mount with the parable of the builders to underline the importance of action. Those who hear but do not act are like the man who built on the instability of sand. The ones who hear truth and act on it, build the structure of their lives on rock.

I am convinced that the reason prayer becomes shallow and eventually hollow is because we resist the follow-through required. Often we return with the same personality difficulties because we were shown things about our character which required change and we resisted. Or the costly order for reconciliation or restitution in our relationships was mandated by the Lord and we resisted meliorating it into our behavior. When we return to the Lord in prayer, reiterating the same needs, He says, "Act on what I told you to do before and I will give you fresh guidance for the next phase of my unfolding strategy for you."

This outline of prayer is a guide for daily prayer. It follows the essential outline of prayer given in the Lord's Prayer and is offered in response to the human plea, "How can I maximize my prayers?" Each week I receive hundreds of letters from our church's national TV audience. Among them are always dozens who ask how to pray. And beneath different expressions of need is the longing to know how to listen to the Lord and share our deepest concerns with Him. I suggest at least fifteen minutes each day for these eight steps of prayer. They have been the lifeline for my prayers. I long for nothing less for you. Utilize them when you're at your best, morning or evening. Combine them with daily reading of the Bible. Then brief prayers can be added all through the day in each situation, problem, or opportunity. A prolonged time, not less than fifteen minutes, does not substitute for praying all through the day. How to do that, making all of life a prayer, is the awesome privilege awaiting us in the next chapter.

Note

1. Author unknown.

For Further Thought . . .

1. "God wants to shape our desires as He guides us to pray." In what ways may God shape your desires?

2. List some of the many reasons why we are admonished to begin our prayers with adoration to God.

3. Define *confession*. What in your life stands between you and God? Will you ask God the Holy Spirit to show you those areas yet needing to be confessed?

4. Specifically, how has God blessed you most when you were showing thanks to Him? What is the result of being thankful for all God has done for you?

CHAPTER THREE
WHAT A WONDERFUL WAY TO LIVE!

A man came to see me about how to handle the mounting pressure in his life. I knew he believed in God, so I asked him to tell me about his prayer life. He told me that he had decided years ago to spend a period each morning in prayer and Bible study. "It just doesn't last through the day!" he said. "And things are so harried at work that there's no time to get away from it all to pray."

"Why not pray your way through the day right on the job?" I responded. He said he didn't think that would be possible with people around him all the time. Then I described the secret of prayer without ceasing and how to retreat into the living center of his own soul sanctuary.

"You think with people around, don't you?" I asked.

"I'd better," he laughed, "or I'd lose my job!"

"Then why not also pray?" I asked.

We talked about the power of brief arrows of prayer for wisdom, guidance, and help. I suggested that he send an arrow of prayer to God for the people, problems, and perplexities which were causing him tension. When things got tough, all he needed to do was claim that the Lord was present with him, that He was as concerned about carrying on a conversation with him there at work as He was in the quiet early morning hours when he had his devotions.

"Think of it this way," I suggested. "One hundred ten and a fourth hours make one weak. Spell week, w-e-a-k."

"What do you mean?" the man asked, his interest piqued.

"Well," I said, "you have one hundred and sixty eight hours at your disposal every week—seven times twenty-four, right?" He agreed to the obvious, with a smile. "You sleep about eight hours a night," I continued, "so subtract fifty-six from that and you have one hundred and twelve left. Now you tell me you spend about fifteen minutes in prayer every morning—that's an hour and three fourths each week. Subtract that and you have one hundred and ten and one-fourth hours left uninspired by communion with the Lord and unprotected by His guidance and care. No wonder you're living under pressure," I said urgently. "The hours at work where you're in the bind of impossible schedules and difficult people are unclaimed for the Lord."

I explained that Christ is the Lord of all life, that for Him there is no division between the sacred and the secular. In fact the word "secular" comes from the Latin root *saecularis,* meaning "of the now, belonging to this age." Every "now" moment is sacred to the Lord. His wisdom can be given for our thinking about problems and opportunities, and His guidance is available for our moment-by-moment decisions. Then we talked about how to pray for each person as we talk to them or deal with them. In each problem-solving challenge we can pray, "Lord, I live with the results of so many poor decisions and wrong choices. Help me right now to think clearly and see all the facts of this complication. Show me what to be, do, and say."

The man's face brightened. He got the picture of living in the flow of supernatural power all through the unclaimed hundred and ten and a fourth hours at work, at home, at church, and in the community that had not been filled with the power of prayer. His response expressed excitement and the desire to experiment with praying all through the day. So I continued about prayer at night.

"And here's a way to claim those fifty-six night hours. Go to sleep praying. Ask the Lord to work in your mind all through the night and He will. You'll awake refreshed and have ideas and solutions that the day hours will demand."

"What a wonderful way to live!" my friend exclaimed.

"The only way to live adventuresomely and abundantly," I rejoined.

Marcus Aurelius once said, "The soul is dyed with the color of its leisure thoughts." I'd say that the soul is dyed with the color of our momentary thoughts all through the day. The author of Proverbs was right, "As we think in our hearts, so are we" (see Prov. 23:7). We become what we think about all the time and if the Lord is given access to our thoughts in only a brief time of prayer each day, we will become less than the persons He intends us to be. J.M. Barrie said, "To have faith is to have wings." Wings of prayer lift us above the present pressures so we can get perspective and receive power to be maximum for the Lord.

Wherever I go, people tell me that their greatest problem is living out their faith in the daily round of activities and challenges. So often they express the desire to get away from it all to rediscover their relationship with the Lord. Now I'm a firm believer in retreats for spiritual renewal and times away alone for prayer and planning. But these times can only strengthen us to discover the resources of prayer for the daily demands of living. It's what happens to us in the battle which shapes our lives.

Morning quiet times are absolutely essential to go

through the steps of effective prayer we talked about in
the previous chapter, but it's throughout the day that we
need the Lord to unfold the specific implications of His
will. And He's ever ready to help. "God is our refuge and
strength, a very present help in trouble. Therefore we will
not fear . . . The Lord of hosts is with us" (Ps. 46:1-2,7).
That is what Archbishop William Trench claimed when he
said, "Prayer is not overcoming God's reluctance; it is lay-
ing hold on His highest willingness."

We all want what I like to call the three *E*s of abundant
living: Energy, Efficiency, and Endurance. We long to
receive the energy of the Holy Spirit for our needs; we
want to use the energies efficiently for His glory and our
growth as persons; and we want to endure when the going
gets rough. The Apostle Paul gives us three admonitions
which cover all these needs in our lives. They cover the
whenever, wherever, and whatever of our experience of
praying through all our hours. Here is a practical, biblical
guide for making all of life a prayer:

Whenever: "Pray without ceasing" (1 Thess. 5:17).

Wherever: "Therefore, I desire that the men pray everywhere, lifting up holy hands, without wrath and
doubting" (1 Tim. 2:8).

Whatever: "Rejoice in the Lord always. Again I will say,
rejoice! Let your gentleness be known to all men.
The Lord is at hand. Be anxious for nothing, but in
everything by prayer and supplication, with thanksgiving, let your requests be made known to God; and
the peace of God, which surpasses all understanding,
will guard your hearts and minds through Christ
Jesus" (Phil. 4:4-7).

I want to consider each of these with you, plumbing
the depths of what they can mean in specific application.

Whenever of Prayer

First, the "whenever" of prayer. We are invited to talk to the Lord and listen to Him to draw on His energy, efficiency, and endurance all the time, in all places, and in all circumstances. Some penetrating questions are helpful. Is there any time when God is unavailable? Is there any place where He is not? Is there any circumstance we could handle better without Him? Experience has taught us to answer all these questions with an emphatic "no!" Prayer without ceasing is built on that strong conviction.

Commenting on Paul's admonition for continuous prayer, Alexander McLaren, that great Scottish expositor of another generation, said, "A very high ideal, but a very reasonable one, for unless we can find some place where God is not, and where the telegraph between heaven and earth are beyond reach, there is no place where we should not pray. And unless we can find a place where we do not want God, nor need Him, there is no place where we should not pray. Because, then, everywhere is equally near Him, and the straight road to His throne is all the same length from every hole and corner of the world; therefore wherever people are, they ought to be clinging to His skirts."[1]

The challenge to pray whenever, in all times, becomes not only a source of strength for every moment, but also a good basis of making our choices about life-style and associations. Must God be excluded? Then it's best not to do it! Have we planned our life so cautiously that we're not attempting soul-sized challenges which only His power could help us achieve? Then life has lost its gusto. Are we spending our hours in things in which we'd be embarrassed to include the Lord? Then we've lived with the illusion that we have the power to exclude Him. The psalmist put it pointedly. "I have set the Lord always before me; because He is at my right hand I shall not be moved" (Ps. 16:8).

Paul lived his own advice to pray without ceasing. He claimed the companionship of prayer in victory, defeat, uncertainty, sickness, and persecution. Each move in his missionary journeys was guided by the Lord. He battled for faith alone as the basis of righteousness with the leaders of Israel as well as the Church; he communicated the gospel with freshness in each unique situation and to different types of personalities; he ministered relentlessly with supernatural strength; he confronted the resistance of friends and enemies; he was relentless in his purpose in triumph and tragedy. And the secret was that he was in constant communion with the Lord. From his decisive encounter with the Lord on the road to Damascus to his imprisonment in Rome, the reason for his spectacular life was: "All I care for is to know Christ, to experience the power of his resurrection" (Phil. 3:10, *NEB*).

"Whenever" prayer opens every moment to the resources of the Lord. He offers us His gifts: grace, faith, wisdom, discernment, and insight. The fruit of the Spirit is provided. Love, joy, peace, longsuffering, kindness, goodness, faithfulness, gentleness, self-control (Gal. 5:22-23). We need never be lonely for we are never alone.

Wherever of Prayer

Now claim these resources in the "wherever" of prayer. Based on his own experiences of the omnipresence and omniscience of his ubiquitous, ever-present Lord, Paul challenged people to pray everywhere. That covers the whole range of life's experiences. Alone, with people, at home, on the job, making money or making love, on vacation or in the battles of life. Psalm 139 describes David's

All through the day I try to remember to breathe out the prayer, "Lord, I need you!" and then breathe in with the prayer of receptive gratitude, "Lord, I receive you!"

experience of the "everywhereness" of the Lord. "Where can I go from Your Spirit? Or where can I flee from Your presence? If I ascend into heaven, You are there; if I make my bed in hell, behold, You are there. If I take the wings of the morning, and dwell in the uttermost parts of the sea, even there Your hand shall lead me, and Your right hand shall hold me. If I say, 'Surely the darkness shall fall on me,' even the night shall be light about me; indeed, the darkness shall not hide from You, but the night shines as the day; the darkness and the light are both alike to You" (Ps. 139:7-12). The Lord of all life is not only always available for prayer, but He is inescapable. And in each moment He is calling us into prayer so that His best can be given to us and the people around us.

I find it helpful to think of prayer everywhere like breathing. All through the day I try to remember to breathe out the prayer, "Lord, I need you!" and then breathe in with the prayer of receptive gratitude, "Lord, I receive You!" It works wonders while studying or writing, talking with people, in staff or official board meetings, as well as in trying times of difficulty. Our minds are amazingly capable of doing several things at the same time. In a conversation, for example, we do not deny another person our full attention when at the same time we are praying for him or her. The same is true for preaching. While I am speaking I try to remember to pray all through the message that what is said will reach people's minds and hearts. When people listen and pray for what God wants to tell them through the message, powerful things happen. And the glory goes to the Lord!

A further aspect of Paul's word to Timothy that we should pray everywhere is that we should lift "holy hands without wrath or doubting." The Hebrew practice of lifting hands when in prayer, mentioned in the Old Testament

(Neh. 8:6), is probably what Paul referred to. The practice is customary in some churches today. I've found it to be a helpful and tangibly physical way of claiming the Lord's presence and power in various situations in which I pray for help.

The other day I was on a long flight from coast to coast. The hours had to be spent in a very strategic study and writing assignment. The need for clarity and accuracy was demanding. Often through the hours I would put my pen down, lift my arms and pray silently, "Lord, help me!" Later during the mealtime a woman across the aisle leaned over and said, "Sir, are you alright? You seem to be stretching a lot."

I laughed as I told her, "Yes, I was stretching, but also praying." She seemed interested in this gesture of prayer so I explained that what I was writing needed the Lord's word-for-word guidance and inspiration. That led to a visit about prayer and the Lord's intervening power in our affairs.

Just as the plane landed, she looked me in the eye and said, "I need you to do some stretching for me. I've got some difficult decisions to make in the next few days. Pray for me. And after what I've learned about prayer in our talk, you can be sure I'll be praying for the Lord's help. People in my office will probably think I'm stretching a lot also!" We both laughed and she went off to meet her particular set of impossibilities in which I am confident she discovered that with the Lord's intervention, all things are possible.

A friend of mine is a famous surgeon. He's also a committed Christian who believes that his skill is a gift of the Lord. The spiritual gift of healing is coupled with immense capabilities as a surgeon. One day in the operating room, a relatively new assistant asked him a question. "Why is it that at the most strategic, life-and-death moment of the surgery you pause, put down your instruments and stretch?" He explained that in tedious operations like that he needed the Great Physician's help and he paused to pray that he would know the exact thing to do. This brilliant surgeon had learned that the Lord was with him and his powers were dependent on His guidance.

I have another friend who leans back in his chair and lifts his hands at crisis points in meetings in the board room of his company. He is praying for wisdom. His associates are aware that his most ingenious suggestions are made after one of those "stretching times."

We needn't press that gesture of supplication too far. The Lord is no more available if we lift our hands in claiming His help. What is important is developing a technique of praying in all circumstances, everywhere.

Whatever of Prayer

That leads us to Paul's *third admonition to pray in all things*. This is the "whatever" of continuous prayer. "Be anxious for nothing, but in everything, by prayer and supplication, with thanksgiving, let your requests be made known to God" (Phil. 4:6). This is what George Tyrell called "a life of friendship with God." In this friendship we can depend on the Lord to be with us in whatever happens. All we have to do to realize His intervention is to take the feeling of anxiety as the signal to pray. When we talk to the Lord in the midst of the opportunity or challenge, we are to relinquish the management of the problem or potential to Him and thank Him for it.

You're probably thinking, "Listen, Lloyd, there are lots of things for which I'd find it difficult to thank the Lord!" I know that it is not easy to thank the Lord for troublesome people and turbulent problems. And yet, if we believe that

In all the dimensions of living life as a prayer, the greater result with be that we will come to know and love our God more profoundly as a friend.

the Lord is in charge, we can be sure that He will use what happens to us for what He wants to happen to and through us. Thanking Him in advance of solutions sets us free to discover what He may want to teach us. So often we look back at tough times and realize that we grew the most in the midst of them. The five words for a motto of victorious living are "Thank the Lord in trouble." When we do, we are released from the tension of facing it alone. The peace Paul talks about flows into our hearts.

In all the whenever, wherever, and whatever dimensions of living life as a prayer, the purpose is not just to get out of difficulties or solve problems or deal with troublesome people. All that will happen, but the greater result will be that we will come to know and love our God more profoundly as a friend. Not just in formal prayer times, but in the flow of life. Albert Day expressed that assurance. "This is the meaning of prayer—not to get things but to realize God. This is the greatest answer to prayer—not bread nor healing nor guidance, but companionship, Divine—human companionship."

One of the reasons I appreciate the poetry of Annie Johnson Flint so much is that it was written in physical pain. And yet she knew the Lord with an intimacy we all desire. Here's the reason.

> I dare not pray for any gift
>   Upon my pilgrim path to heaven;
> I only ask one thing of Thee
>   Give Thou Thyself, and all is given.[2]

Pray that prayer wherever, whenever, and in whatever life brings each day, and those one hundred and ten and one-fourth hours we talked about will make you strong. Indeed, what a wonderful way to live!

Note

1. Alexander McLaren, *Expositions of Holy Scriptures* (Grand Rapids: Baker Book House, 1975), vol. 15, p. 354.
2. Annie Johnson Flint, "My Prayer," *Flint's Best Loved Poems* (Grand Rapids: Zondervan Publishing House, n.d.), p. 86.

For Further Thought . . .

1. Times of prayer are called spiritual retreats. Do you currently go on spiritual retreats? There are many workable settings for these spiritual retreats, such as your own bedroom, sitting out under the apple tree or watching the waves roll in on the beach. Name other settings. What are your favorite times and places for spiritual retreats?

2. List the three E's of abundant living. How does each relate to your prayer life?

3. We should be able to communicate with God in all places and circumstances. Are there areas in your life where you would be embarrassed to include Him?

4. In what areas do you find it hard to give God thanks? What five words make up the motto of victorious living? Why does our author suggest you adopt this motto for the hard times?

CHAPTER FOUR

The Transforming Power of Prayer

The other day, as I was driving along in my car, my attention was arrested by a billboard. In bold, black letters it said, "Prayer changes things!" I thought a lot about that as I drove along. Does prayer change things? Well, yes and no. Certainly, when we pray God does intervene and make a difference in circumstances. But at the center of most of the difficulties and problems we face are people. Usually the way God changes things is to change those people. And yet, one of the greatest miracles of prayer is how God changes us and then frees us to cooperate with Him in changing people. Wonderful things begin to happen when, through prayer, we allow Him to change our attitudes toward the people and problems we face.

I want to communicate an astounding promise in this chapter. *We don't have to remain as we are.* We have been programmed for progress. William James said, "The most exciting discovery of our generation is that we can alter our person by altering our attitudes." Prayer is how it happens. There is a transforming power in prayer. George Bernard Shaw said, "Those who cannot change their minds cannot change anything." Prayer can be a mighty force in changing our minds about the people for whom we are concerned or distressed.

Look at it this way. When we have problems which are hassling our peace of mind, as we have said, the Lord instigates in us a desire to pray. We tell Him all about the problem and ask for His guidance. Or we are troubled about some person: a loved one who is in need, a friend whose life-style disturbs us, a fellow worker who doesn't measure up, or a neighbor who upsets us by the way he or she lives. Again the Lord is the initiator of the desire to pray about these people. Often we think that because we pray we can dispatch the Lord to straighten out these people according to the detailed specifications we have outlined to Him. When the answer isn't immediate, we wonder if He's heard us. Then a wonderful thing begins to happen. Our attitude of worry, judgment, impatience, or defensiveness begins to change. We begin to feel differently about the people. We see them through the eyes of our Lord. We feel love, understanding, and compassion. Often it is our changed attitude which gives them the desire to change. And even if they remain the same, we are able to cope much more effectively because of the transformation of our attitudes. We can't change most situations or people, until the Lord changes us. Changed people change situations around them. Beginning with them.

How does this happen? Paul tells us the secret in his second letter to the Corinthians. Though the word *prayer* is not mentioned in the passage I have in mind, it is really a description of how the Lord changes us, our attitudes, and subsequently, our relationships with people. It is through prayer that we appropriate this promise. "Now the Lord is the Spirit; and where the Spirit of the Lord is, there is liberty. But we all, with unveiled face, beholding as in a mirror the glory of the Lord, are being transformed into the same image from glory to glory, just as by the Spirit of the

Lord" (2 Cor. 3:17-18). Paul has given us the *purpose* of prayer, the transforming *power* of prayer, and the *promise* of prayer.

The Purpose of Prayer

The purpose of prayer is communion with the Lord who is the Spirit. "Now the Lord is the Spirit." The unity of Christ and the Holy Spirit is affirmed. The same Christ who came from the heart of God in the incarnation, returns to us in the Spirit to take up residence in us. Prayer is intimate communication in what Thomas Kelly called the divine center in each of us. It is from within us that the Lord does His work of changing us.

The task of the indwelling Lord is to introduce us to the real person who lives inside us. We are so much more than the outward person others see. He wants to liberate the unique, distinctly different person each of us is. "Where the Spirit of the Lord is, there is freedom." How does He do it? He told us plainly during His ministry. "If you abide in My word, you are My disciples indeed. And you shall know the truth and the truth will make you free . . . . Therefore if the Son makes you free, you shall be free indeed" (John 8:31-32,36). Jesus is telling us about freedom from sin. But what is sin? Not just the bad things we do, but the bound-up person we are. Sin is to miss the mark of the reason for which each of us was born. It is also the refusal to be the unique miracle each of us is. Christ sets us free from whatever binds the special person inside us.

The Transforming Power of Prayer

But mere liberation would be ineffective if the Lord didn't do something to shape and direct the person who is released. Liberation must be coupled with transformation.

And so Paul goes on. "We all, with unveiled face, beholding as in a mirror the glory of the Lord, are being transformed into the same image from glory to glory" (2 Cor.
3:18). This is in contrast to Moses' experience which the
apostle had explained earlier in the passage. It reveals the
different quality of prayer made possible after the incarnation, resurrection, and Pentecost. Moses' prayers to the
Lord on Mount Sinai produced a radiance on his face. But
the radiance would fade, so he placed a veil over his face
so that the people would not see the diminishing radiance.
Paul shows the difference in us as a result of the transforming power of prayer. Our communion with the Lord is
meant to be consistent and constant; therefore the glory
manifested in our personalities and on our countenances
does not fade.

We are transformed by beholding. Prayer is beholding.
And what do we behold? Paul's words can be interpreted
in two ways. Beholding in a mirror the glory of the Lord
can mean that we gaze into the gospel and behold Christ,
who is the image of God. It may also mean something else.
The Greek word used here for "beholding in a mirror" is a
compound participle. *Katoptrizomenoi* is the present middle participle of *katoptrizō*, a verb from the noun *katoptron*,
meaning "a mirror to see with"—*Kata*, with; *optron*, see.

The question is what Paul meant. What is reflected in
the mirror into which we look? One meaning is that we
behold the glory of God reflected in the face of Jesus
Christ. Beholding Him we grow in His likeness. Another
possible interpretation is that we are allowed to see our
own faces with the glory of the Lord manifested on them.
This second idea holds more closely to the Greek word for
mirror. I think Paul mixed his metaphors and implied both
meanings. Surely the whole thrust of the passage is that
we have been given the privilege of beholding God face to

In prayer we behold the glory of Christ as we commune with Him. His glory in our hearts transforms us from within. We are changed into His likeness.

face in Christ the Mediator.

"Glory" in Hebrew is *kabod* meaning value, weight, substance. When applied to God who is a Spirit the word *glory* is synonymous with the splendor of His presence and power. In Greek the word means manifestation. *Doxa* means the Lord's revelation of His nature and attributes. That's why the Scriptures speak of Christ as the glory of God. This is what Paul means when, a few verses later in chapter 4, he says, "For it is the God who commanded light to shine out of darkness who has shown in our hearts to give the light of the knowledge of the glory of God in the face of Jesus Christ" (v. 6). God who brought the light of day out of darkness in creation has illuminated our hearts with the knowledge and experience of His glory in Christ.

In prayer we behold the glory of Christ as we commune with Him. His glory in our hearts transforms us from within. We are changed into His likeness. The Greek word for transformation is *metamorphoō*. It means that there is a change which brings about a congruity between the inner and outer dimensions of our personalities. What's inside is manifested in character, action, attitude, and personality characteristics. We do not experience transformation by beholding the person we were, but by beholding Christ. But the exciting implication of the mirror metaphor may be that the Lord gives us the encouragement of being able to see the change as we look into the mirror and realize that beholding Him has made us progressively more and more like Him. This is hinted at in the *Living Bible* paraphrase of 2 Corinthians 3:18. "But we Christians have no veil over our faces; we can be mirrors that brightly reflect the glory of the Lord. And as the Spirit of the Lord works within us, we become more and more like Him." Could it be that the Lord also allows us the delight of seeing the change He is manifesting in us? Does

He enjoy sharing the progress with us? I am convinced He does.

Dr. F. B. Meyer put it clearly. "We reflect. The beauty of His face glancing on ours will be mirrored, as a man's eye will contain a tiny miniature picture of what he is beholding. Then we will be changed. If you try to represent Jesus in your character and behavior, you will become transfigured into His likeness. Love makes like. Imitation produces assimilation."[1]

What does all this mean to you and me and our discovery of how to pray with power? Everything! The Lord creates in us the desire to pray because He wants to make us like Himself. As we take time to be with Him in prayer we feel loved and affirmed. The result is not pride or complacency; strangely, it produces a desire to grow in Christlikeness. It isn't that we work out an idea of the person we want to be and then get His help to fulfill our plans. Rather, as we come to know Him better, changes take place inadvertently. In the pure light of His presence, we see ourselves as we are. We could not endure that experience if it were not for the fact that honesty about ourselves is enabled by His unlimited love.

We all want to press on in becoming mature men and women in Christ. It's a serious thing. I've never met a person who is totally satisfied with the man or woman he or she is. Whatever accomplishments we achieve, there is an inherent longing to press on. We are like the artist who was asked, "What is your greatest painting?" He responded, "The next one!" We'd all echo that about any project, day, or phase of our lives. Complete satisfaction with ourselves seems to be a luxury the Lord has decided to deny us so that we might press on in becoming more of the person He created us to become.

The amazing thing is the way the Lord works with us.

He does not plunge us into inordinate dissatisfaction or force us to be protectively defensive about ourselves. He does not allow us to get down on ourselves or be proud of our progress. In the ambience of His love we are shown things which cripple our freedom to be creative communicators of His love to others. His way of dealing with us is radically different from the current self-realization therapies of our time. He has a much greater purpose: His desire is to make us people who can be channels of His affirmation, assurance, forgiveness, and new life to others. In keeping with that, the thrust of the New Testament about the need for character transformation is always in the context of our calling to be ambassadors of hope, agents of reconciliation, and stewards of the manifold grace of the Lord. Whatever gets in the way is what the Lord wants to change in us. To do that He communicates forgiveness for what we've been and a vivid picture of what we can become.

Just the opposite of the way Christ works in us was depicted in a cartoon I saw recently. I like cartoons. They make me laugh at myself and, sometimes, even think. Ed Frascino is one of my favorite cartoonists. He loves to poke fun at "that stagnant, bound together with another person thing" of some middle-aged couples. One of his cartoons depicting that caught my attention. A grim, hatchet-faced woman was seated next to her equally grim, overbearing, and overweight husband. As she glared critically, she said, "What's your biggest fault and what are you going to do about it?"

That question is often implied, if not asked, in lots of relationships—by young and old, single and married. The last thing most of us need is to contemplate our faults without an atmosphere of affirmation in which we are encouraged to grow as persons. When another person is

In prayer He activates our imagination to picture the person we long to be by His transforming power and then offers us the help we need.

over against us with negative criticism we become rigidly intractable.

How differently Christ deals with us! His question is not, "What is your greatest fault and what are you going to do about it?" but "What would you be like if you allowed me to form your character and personality like mine?" In prayer He activates our imagination to picture the person we long to be by His transforming power and then offers us the help we need. He does that by removing the barriers to Christlikeness. Most of us are haunted with fears. These shape our personalities into inverted, cautious distortions. He helps us look at these one by one. Then He deals with the memories which lurk within—the times we failed, were hurt by others, or stunted in our personality growth by the debilitating experiences during the early years of our lives. The Lord allows us to look honestly at what our parents and our families did to encourage or discourage our emergence as self-accepting, life-affirming people capable of receiving and giving love. As we probe deeper with His loving guidance in prayer, He helps us receive and give forgiveness. Memories are expunged of their poison.

Now the Lord is ready to deal with habit patterns in our attitudes. Why do we react the way we do? What causes us to respond to some people and reject others? What lack of security in His love makes us negatively critical, judgmental, or hostile?

Consistently in prayer with the Lord we can look back over the previous day and affirm progress and question the deeper causes of any lack of freedom. He gently, but persistently, touches the raw nerve of the deeper causes.

Throughout the lifelong process of creative personality prayer therapy, as we are ready, subconscious repressions

will surface and can be dealt with in conversation with the
Lord. We will become progressively more liberated. We
will find that we enjoy the person who lives in our skin and
befriend his or her struggle to be whole. The delightful,
evolving result is that we will begin to love ourselves as
we are loved by the Lord. As Dr. Karen Horney explains,
"The feeling of being loved and even more of being love-
able is perhaps one of the greatest values in life." And one
of the primary purposes of prayer is to give us the gift of
both with the added plus of wanting to communicate both
to the people around us.

In explaining this process of the transformation of personality through prayer, I do not want to negate the function of the trained Christian psychologist or psychiatrist.
Often we need help in understanding what has conditioned
and shaped our personalities. But even when the Lord
uses another person to help us, eventually we must deal
with the discoveries and insights ourselves in our relationship with Him. We cannot see ourselves as we are or gain
a true picture of what we can become without His love and
the strength for behavior modification.

Another source of help are Christian friends who will
listen to us as we grapple with our assets and liabilities.
Often prayer groups reach the level of intimacy in which
we can talk out what the Lord is showing us about ourselves. When the action step of change is mandated, we
need the prayers of others to spur us on. I have never
been without a group like that. Presently I am in a group of
fellow adventurers in growth in Christ. The participants
communicate, listen, and give me courage to dare to grow
and change. I can trust them because I know they too are
on a personality pilgrimage of being formed into the image
of Christ.

The Promise of Prayer

All this that I tried to share about prayer and personality in this chapter comes down to some personal questions. Have you ever thought of prayer as the dynamic communion with the Lord in which He seeks to transform you into His likeness? If so, are you presently yielding who you are to His healing and reformation? Have you ever asked Him to show you your full potential as His person? Do you dare to yield to His molding Spirit the future development of your personality?

"Therefore, if anyone is in Christ, he is a new creation; old things have passed away; behold, all things have become new" (2 Cor. 5:17). And for what purpose? To love as we've been loved! Prayer doesn't just change things. It changes us.

> Lord, what a change within us one short hour
> Spent in Thy presence will prevail to make!
> What heavy burdens from our bosoms take,
> What parched grounds refresh as with a shower!
> We kneel, and all around us seems to lower;
> We rise, and all, the distant and the near,
> Stands forth in sunny outline brave and clear;
> We kneel, how weak! we rise, how full of power!
> Why, therefore, should we do ourselves this
> wrong,
> Or others, that we are not always strong,
> That we are ever overborne with care,
> That we should ever weak or heartless be,
> Anxious or troubled, when with us is prayer,
> And joy and strength and courage are with Thee![2]

Notes

1. F. B. Meyer, *Great Verses Through the Bible, A Devotional Commentary on Key Verses* (Grand Rapids: Zondervan Publishing House, 1972), p. 427.

2. Richard Chenevix Trench, "Prayer," James Dalton Morrison, ed., *Masterpieces of Religious Verse* (New York: Harper & Row Publishers, 1948), p. 403.

For Further Thought . . .

1. Christians have been "programmed for progress." What tool has God given us to make major transformations in our attitudes? Why is it important for us to be able to change our minds?

2. What is the *purpose* of prayer? What provision has God made for Christians to communicate with Him?

3. Review 2 Corinthians 3:18. How does this verse of Scripture relate to your prayer life?

4. Discuss the questions listed in this chapter under the heading *Promise of Prayer.* Does 2 Corinthians 5:17 describe you?

CHAPTER FIVE

PRAYER AND YOUR WORRIES OVER PEOPLE

Focus in your mind's eye the people about whom you are concerned. The people about whom you worry. Who are they to you? Perhaps you are married to him or her. Maybe you're worried about one of your children. Or it may be a friend who's in trouble, or someone for whom you work or who works for you.

What Is Worry?

I want to share a secret of how to stop worrying about those people and start living. Intercessory prayer can break the worry bind. Worry is thinking turned toxic, concern degenerated into inner conflict. The old English word for worry is *wyrgan* which means to twist or strangle. Worry does that to our love for people. It both twists it into debilitating anxiety and strangles our capacity to discover what to do to help and do it in a way that does not multiply the problem about which we are troubled in another person.

Worry is that anxiety which fills the interface between what is and what we imagine should be. It is the insecure, unstable fill we dump into the caverns excavated by our human expectations. It is the marshy substance that will support no bridge of safe passage; it is the aching memory of what should have been and what should be but seldom is. Worry is unproductive because it is not based on the vision of what God promises He can and will do.

Intercessory Prayer Combats Worry

Intercessory prayer is the antidote to worry over people. But many of us pray for people about whom we are concerned, and still worry. A woman said to me recently, "I pray for my son, but can't seem to stop worrying about him. I talk to God about him and tell Him what my boy needs. But I get up from my knees and soon I am worrying as if I had never prayed." Ever feel like that? How can we pray for people and know that God has heard us, understood, and that He will do something?

Last summer, just before I left for my study leave in Scotland, a friend shared a profound problem he was facing. We spent hours talking it through, then we prayed together, and I departed. I told him I would pray for him each day. The difficulty he was facing was so serious for him and his marriage that I found him coming back to my mind often each day. When I prayed about him it sounded as if I were calling the Lord's attention to a problem about which He had little or no information. Because I thought I knew what the man had to do to save his marriage, I petitioned God almost hourly during the weeks of study and writing. Then one day during a long walk, a reorienting, transforming thought hit me. I had believed that intercessory prayer was my placing my burdens on God's heart. Or at least, that's the way my prayers sounded. Then that day, a totally new conception formed in my mind. It was consistent with the theme the Lord was giving me for this book. It came first as a thought and then was articulated

*The mystery of His
providential care of people is
that He calls us into the
process of His blessing, and
often waits to bless a person
until we pray.*

into words in my mind. It is the secret I must share with you. *Intercessory prayer is God putting His burdens on our hearts.*

Like all prayer, intercessory prayer originates with God, not us. He has wisely decreed that His work will be done in His people cooperatively through the prayers of those on whose hearts He places His burden. If we won't pray, often He won't act. Notice I didn't say that He can't act. He can do anything He wants to do. But the mystery of His providential care of people is that He calls us into the process of His blessing, and often waits to bless a person until we pray.

The word *intercede* in the Latin means "to go or pass between": *inter,* between; *cedere,* go on, pass. The exciting idea the Lord has been giving me is that He is the original, initiating interceder. He intercedes with us, that is, He invades our worry with specific guidance on how to pray for another person. Jesus did that for us in the incarnation and the atonement. And He continues to do that in our prayers. "He ever lives to make intercession for them" (Heb. 7:25), first between us and the heart of God and then into our hearts to give the wisdom of what and how to pray for the people about whom we are tempted to worry.

But so often we worry over a person, finally decide that prayer is our last resort, and then go into God's presence to brief Him on the need and what He should do. Because we feel that it's up to us to persist and that God will bless someone because of the length and repetition of our prayers, we do not get free of the worry. We wonder, Have we said enough? Have we prayed often enough? Is our own life sufficiently in order to deserve an answer to our prayer for a loved one? Now added to our original worry is the concern about the adequacy of our prayers.

We are back in the syndrome of self-justification and bartered love.

It is the Lord who calls us into prayer for people. The thought of a person's need is because He wants to act in that person's life. Part of His strategy is to involve us in His unfolding answer.

I've had some humorous experiences with people's message beepers going off during my preaching. Doctors, and now busy people of all kinds, wear them or carry them in purses. Often they forget to turn down the volume of the beep before coming into worship. Recently, while I was preaching I asked the rhetorical question, "Who in your life needs your love and affirmation?" At that very moment, a doctor's turned-up beeper attached to his belt sounded, invading the quiet of the sanctuary with its loud persistence until the doctor was able to turn it off and leave his pew to return an emergency call from the hospital. The congregation laughed at the timing of my question and the beep. I tried to utilize the unexpected parable and suggested that there was probably a call for help waiting for all of us if we could only hear the plea in people's expressions and the meaning beneath their words. But what if we thought of our concerns over people as a beep from God calling us into prayer? Consider it this way in response:

All that I feel of pity Thou hast known
Before I was; my best is all Thy own
From Thy great heart of goodness mine but drew
Wishes and prayers, but Thou, O Lord, wilt do
In Thine own time, by ways I cannot see,
All that I feel when I am nearest Thee![1]

The impact of this growing understanding of intercessory prayer, subsequent to the insight from the Lord that afternoon as I walked, has broken the worry bind I have experienced so often when people's needs have the potential of starting the cycle of anxiety. The conviction which has gripped me ever since is that it is the Almighty God of power who has called me to join Him in the accomplishment of His plans and purposes for a person.

Look at it this way. If you or I go to a person for help for someone in trouble, the responsibility is ours to convince him or her of the need. Explanation, examples, and appeals to the potential benefactor are made with the hope of touching his or her heart and getting the desired assistance. The burden of proof is ours. Our plea must be convincing enough to motivate action. Even after we've presented the need we are left with the uncertainty about whether we have said the right thing. But most of all, we wonder if the person has the resources to help even after we have marshalled his or her desire to help. That's the way many of us think about intercessory prayer.

Now turn that around totally. Think of being called by someone who wants to help a friend or loved one of ours. There is no need of convincing or impassioned appeals. We are asked to be the mediator and implementor of the help. Our only task is to learn what the person wants to do or give. Our responsibility is not asking, but claiming what is offered. And that's the way our Lord wants us to think about our prayers for others.

Jesus Gave a Model

Jesus' priestly prayer for His disciples on the night before the crucifixion is an excellent model for our intercessory prayers. It's found in the seventeenth chapter of John. Read it over carefully. Note how Jesus reaffirms His oneness with the Father as the basis of His confidence in prayer. His claim and confidence is based on what the Father had already done and declared. Then the Lord prays for the disciples as people given Him by His Father. "I have manifested Your name to the men whom You have given Me out of the world. They were Yours, You gave them to Me, and they have kept Your word. Now they have known that all things which You have given Me are from You" (vv. 6-7). The prayer is more like reporting in for duty and a fresh update of vision already revealed. Jesus goes on to claim all that the Father had promised for the disciples. Then the prayer proceeds to include those who will become believers through the disciples. "I do not pray for these alone, but also for those who will believe in Me through their word; that they all may be one, as You, Father, are in Me, and I in You; that they also may be one in Us, that the world may believe that You have sent Me. And the glory which You gave Me I have given them, that they may be one just as We are one" (vv. 20-22).

The Lord's intercessory prayer was in perfect consistency with what He knew was the heart of God. Our response may be, "Well, Jesus was the Son of God; of course He knew what to pray." And yet, this is the key to unlocking the power of intercessory prayer. Immanuel, God with us, is with us still. Through His Spirit He teaches us what to pray for others. He does that by energizing our imaginations. He gives us a picture of what He wants to do, and then the content of our prayer is to claim that picture. Intercessory prayer is the risen, present Christ continuing His ministry through His chosen and called people.

The exchange between Simon Peter and Jesus in the Upper Room (Luke 22:31-34) helps us to understand the Lord's plans for us as agents of enabling prayers for others. To the then unstable and unconverted disciples He said, "Simon, Simon! Indeed, Satan has asked for you,

that he may sift you as wheat. But I have prayed for you,
that your faith should not fail; and when you have turned to
Me, strengthen your brethren" (Luke 22:31-32). At that
point Peter was not converted, did not have the gift of
faith, and was incapable of ministering to the needs of others. After the resurrection and the empowering of the
indwelling Christ at Pentecost he was converted. "Return
to Me" is a translation of the Greek word *hepistripho,* to
turn, to be transformed, to go in an entirely new direction.
After the effluence of the Spirit at Pentecost, Peter is
given the gift of faith to accept the atonement of the cross,
claim the power of the resurrection, and begin doing what
Jesus did (see John 14:12-14). The interceding prayer
ministry of the incarnate Lord now is carried out by Peter
and the Church. After our conversion our major ministry is
praying for others.

The oft-repeated quote of E.M. Bounds underlines the
crucial calling we have been given. "Talking to men for
God is a great thing, but talking to God for men is greater
still." It is a sublime expression of love. But when we
allow God to talk to us about people, what we have to say
to Him about them in our intercessory prayers is infused
with His love and His wisdom.

The priestly prayer of Jesus gives us further insight in
how to pray when we are concerned for others. The ultimate prayer is that "they may be one." That oneness with
God is the deepest need in everyone for whom we pray.
Oneness means love, communion, intimacy, closeness.
The essential "I" meets the eternal God. Whatever need
in a person drives us to our knees is insignificant in comparison to this. And when we are led to pray about a specific problem, our supreme concern is that the Lord will
use what is happening to a person for introduction to a
deeper relationship with Him.

The reconciliation He died and rose to provide, and returned to impart, is both vertical and horizontal: it is with God and between us and others.

Why God Needs Our Prayers

Having said all this, a question still lingers. Why does God need our prayers? If He knows what is best for someone, why doesn't He just do it without involving us? That's the other dimension of the oneness Jesus prayed for. He came not only to make us one with God, but to call us into oneness with each other. The reconciliation He died and rose to provide, and returned to impart, is both vertical and horizontal: it is with God and between us and others. That's why intercessory prayer is so crucial. The Lord wants us to be to one another what He has been to us in love, forgiveness, and unlimited concern. The mystery of it all is that often He will not bless another until we pray. When we do pray, His love flows through us to the other person. The help the Lord has reserved until we prayed is given because we have become agents of His intervention. When He is ready to give reconciliation, salvation, healing, strength, guidance, or the resolution of a seemingly unsolvable problem, He enlists us into partnership for the accomplishment of His will.

That is both a source of awe and a reason for alarm. The fact that God has decided to bless through the prayers of His people is humbling. But it is also startling when we realize how little time and effort we expend in intercessory prayer. We wonder about who in our lives may be enduring less than God's maximum because we have not taken our calling seriously. Saint Francis de Sales put it this way: "God did not deprive thee of the operation of His love, but thou didst deprive Him of thy cooperation."

Added to that, many relationships remain on a mediocre level because we pray so little for others. Nothing engenders love and delight over the unique miracle which each person is more than prayer. William Law said, "Intercession is the best arbitration of differences, the best promoter of true friendship, the best cure and preservative agent against unkind tongues, all anger and haughty passion." Intercessory prayer frees us to love the persons for whom we pray. We feel the pulsebeat of the Lord's love. Concern for them prompts forgiveness and patience. Our hearts are knit to theirs as we claim what the Lord has given us—the discernment and boldness to ask for them. We are on their side—for them. People desperately need that. God knows—He created us so that we could not be complete without Him or each other. Intercession is the mother tongue of the new creation in Christ.

And yet we've all prayed for people who have resisted what seemed to be best for them. We all have free will and some of the people for whom we pray are in what Luther called the "bondage of the will." There are times when people resist receiving what the Lord has prompted us to ask. That's a signal for our prayers to plunge deeper. The will can dominate both thought and emotion. People can will not to accept the Lord's blessing. The will is released from bondage of the imperious self-control only by the invasion of the Spirit of the Lord. No one decides to want God until He creates the desire in him or her. When a person is resistant, pray for the liberation of the will and trust that the gift of faith will be given. When God puts that need on our hearts, it is because that's exactly what He desires and is preparing to do.

Worry Is a Substitute for Intercession

A concern for a person is a call to intercessory prayer. Worry is a substitute for intercession. And worrying after we've prayed is a sure sign that we think of prayer as our effort and that perhaps God has not heard. Added to that, it is a lack of trust. And that may tell us more about our need than the person for whom we are praying. Worry is a cycle of unproductive thought whirling around a center of hidden fear. We cannot receive the cure of our worry until we allow the Lord to show us what fear in us is causing it. Perhaps we fear losing control or want to direct another person's life. Claiming that God is in charge may be very frightening. Or we may have asked the Lord for something in our own lives and it has not come on our timing or to our specifications. We have little confidence that He will hear us in our concerns for others any more than we think He hears us about our own set of problems. Worry is the natural result of unbelief.

Worry Becomes a Habit

The problem is that worry becomes a habit. After a while, we need it to feel secure. We are like dope addicts needing a fix. We can actually create situations about which we can worry. What can we do? The cure of worry is not just the belief that things will work out for good under the providence of God. It comes from wrenching our egos from the throne of our hearts. Worry is a manifestation that we are still living with our wills in control and our desires as the focus of our prayers. The worry syndrome is seldom broken until we are willing to be called into prayer to receive God's orders for what is best rather than tenaciously grasping what we are determined to convince Him should be done. Helmut Thielicke said, "Care can be cured only by care. Care about many things can be cured only by care about the one thing needful. This is the homeopathy of divine healing." And the one thing needful? Jesus said it was to seek first God's kingdom and all else would be given. The creative fear of missing the reason we were born displaces all secondary fears. When we put

God first in our lives, people and their needs become a close second. The ministry of prayer is not an option for those so inclined by nature. Our new nature in Christ is manifested in the willingness to be called by Him into a ministry of listening for what we are to pray for others, and then responding by asking with boldness for those things He has clarified.

Desire to Become Involved

A further result of consistent intercessory prayer is that we are given a desire to become involved in the implementation of our prayers. When we have listened to the Lord to discover His strategy, often He gives us marching orders for practical assistance which we can be to the person for whom we have prayed. Armed with profound discernment we know what to do and say. All that we've been given of insight, wisdom, experience, and material resources can then be deployed to be the Lord's love in action.

A word of caution needs to be sounded about telling people the result of our listening prayers for them. When the Lord gives us wisdom on how to pray, we should be very thoughtful about going to a person to say, "The Lord has told me what you ought to do!" When that takes on the freight of our determination to gain control over a person it can be very dangerous. However, just as the Lord gives us guidance in how to pray for a person, He also will give us the signal of if and when to share an insight. We need to wait and watch for a receptivity in people. That usually is the result of our caring for them in very practical and supportive ways. Earning the right to be heard, coupled with the Lord's timing, is a winning combination.

The other day, I overheard a conversation. One man said to his friend, "I've been praying for you." The quick retort of the other man was, "Thanks, but tell me—what did you pray? Hope you're not like some of my friends who tell me they have a pipeline to heaven and tell God exactly what I ought to do. The problem is that they all have conflicting guidance. If I followed them I'd go off in all directions." Sensing the bristled spirit in the man, the intercessor said, "The conviction I get as I pray for you is that God loves you very much, knows the bind you're in, and will not leave or forsake you." I learned that later when the man was ready to talk, he called on this wise, sensitive and affirming friend. The faithful intercessor let him talk for a long time. When the troubled man got around to a possible solution which was close to what he had been led by the Lord to pray for, he gently responded, "I think you're on target. That fits with what I've sensed the Lord is trying to say in your need." I like that!

Of course, there are times when we are so convicted about a danger in another person's direction that we must share our concern candidly. But not without the preparation of becoming a loving friend. People resist those who try to straighten them out. There are people in my life who have communicated their faithfulness. I will listen when the Lord has guided them to intercede for me in a particular direction. Like most of us, I am put off by people who get into a power struggle with me and use the fact that they are praying for me as a hammer to tell me what to do. However, when they have become trusted friends, I seek their counsel which has been honed in prolonged intercessory prayer for me.

The issue raised about intercessory prayer is whether our prayers for others make any difference. Often we ask: Can our prayers change God's will for a person? Can our sincere wish alter the counsel of the Almighty? What I have tried to communicate in this chapter is that those questions indicate we are missing the purpose of intercessory prayer. The real question is: Can God implant in our minds the maximum expression of His will for another person? Can we cooperate with Him in the accomplishment of His will by praying for him or her? Yes! And when we receive that and respond in our prayers, we become essential agents for the Lord to pour out His blessings. Oneness with Him and the persons for whom we pray will result. We can stop worrying and start living!

Note

1. Author unknown.

For Further Thought . . .

1. List some of the things you tend to worry about. What is the antidote God provides to combat worry?

2. There are times when we feel the need to pray for others. Why is that? What kind of prayer is this? Who is our model for this type of prayer?

3. Who has God laid on your heart recently to pray for? What do you envision for that person in your prayers? Can you boldly claim for that person what God has put on your heart to pray for?

4. Why is intercessory prayer so important? How much time do you spend praying for others?

CHAPTER SIX

THE QUESTION OF UNANSWERED PRAYER

Some time ago I gave a series of messages on prayer to my congregation in Hollywood, California. One Sunday morning, as I greeted the people after one of these messages, a woman pressed a carefully folded note into the palm of my hand. She held my hand firmly as I looked into her eyes long enough to know that whatever was written on the note was urgent and the expression of an honest need. I thanked her for it and assured her that as soon as I had finished with the greeting I would read it and respond.

When I reached my study and had a few leisurely moments to unfold the note, this is what I read: "Lloyd, I have appreciated all the positive things you have said about how to pray with power, but I must be very honest. This series on prayer has made me feel very lonely, even a bit angry at times. I look around me as you tell all the glorious things that happen when we pray and see everyone nodding in agreement and affirmation. Doesn't anyone feel the way I do about those times when prayer is unanswered? Here's my problem. For months now I've had the feeling that God neither heard nor responded to my prayers. I have gone from feelings of guilt that something must be wrong with me, to doubt about whether God cares. I

just had to tell someone—to ask the lurking question—
why are some prayers unanswered?"

Ever feel that way? Have you ever known an excruciating dry spell in your prayers when there seemed to be
no answer to your prayers? Of course, we all have. Deep
down inside of all of us are questions about why prayers
sometimes seem like an endless monologue. In those
times, the enthusiastic witness of others about answered
prayer seems to mock our impatience with God. We listen, not wanting to cloud the sunny skies of others with
the thunderheads of our own doubt. But we do feel like
Thomas Hardy once felt as he saw the joyous fellowship of
praying believers.

> That with this bright believing band
>   I have no claim to be,
> That faith by which my comrades stand
>   Seem fantasies to me
> And mirage-mist their Shining Land
>   Is a strange destiny?[1]

There are some who have never had what they would
call a definite answer to prayer. Others have known the
ecstacy of sweet communion with the Lord in prayer and
have also found that for some strange reason, prayer has
suddenly become sterile and unrewarding. Still others are
like this woman. You have prayed, waited, wondered, and
become weary. And then there are others of us who wres-
tle with the bold promises of the Bible about prayer and
are frustrated by the disparity of what is offered and what
we seem to experience in our prayers. We follow Jesus'
admonition to ask, seek, knock. We read that all we are to
do is make our requests known and they will be granted.
"If you ask anything in My name I will do it," He promises

with assurance. Why then the problem of unanswered prayer?

Helmut Thielicke, the great German theologian and preacher, empathizes with us. "How often have we earnestly pled for something and haven't gotten it? All along the highway of our lives are there not the countless grave-markers of unanswered prayers? Have we not all known bitter disappointment and moments when no voice nor answer came as we ardently prayed, and when we remained alone and disappointed in the silence?"[2]

We answer with an honest "Yes!" But we need more than empathy or the comfort of a shared dilemma. We want to hear from the Lord about why He seems to be silent when we cry out to Him in petitions for the things we earnestly need.

And He is ready. He has dealt with the question before. He opens the way for us to pour out our frustration and then gives us more of an answer than we may have expected!

The other day I talked with a couple who were facing difficulties in communication. The man said, "How I wish I could express my feelings without my wife being defensive. If I could just get out what's happening inside of me in an atmosphere of complete acceptance, not of all that I say, but of me as a person, I know I'd get perspective and be able to change my attitude." That's exactly the kind of openness the Lord creates for us to be able to talk out our frustrations about seemingly unanswered prayer.

The Lord loves us very much. He wants us to express how we are feeling about those times when our prayers seem not to be answered. We don't have to protect His reputation—to ourselves or to others. The question from the deeps of our souls will be answered from the depth of His love. But while we are questioning Him, He may have some very crucial questions to ask us!

That's what happened to Job. The story of Job's suffering is a classic study of the problem of unanswered prayer.
Job was a successful, prosperous man who lost everything—his wealth, children, cattle. Along with these, he
also almost lost his faith in the righteous justice of God.
His friends tried to convince him that he must have sinned
in some way to have brought this punishment from God.
They espoused the belief held at that time that suffering
was the recompense of God for sin. Job protested his innocence. But most acutely he felt the absence of God when
he cried out for vindication. He tried to maintain his belief
in the righteousness of God and his conviction that, if he
could only reach Him, he could question the Almighty
about the injustice he was enduring, and why He would
allow it. Most of all, Job wanted the Lord's presence and
assurance. Listen to Job . . . ever felt as he did?

"Even today my complaint is bitter; my hand is listless
because of my groaning. Oh, that I knew where I might
find Him, that I might come to His seat! I would present
my case before Him, and fill my mouth with arguments. I
would know the words which He would answer me, and
understand what He would say to me. Would He contend
with me in His great power? No! But He would take note
of me. There the upright could reason with Him, and I
would be delivered forever from my Judge" (Job 23:1-7).

Finally, after a prolonged time of what seemed to be no
answer from God to this prayer, Job borders on bitter-
ness. The mocking question of Satan is, "Does Job fear
God for naught?" But the real question is, "Does Job fear
God for God?" When we understand the Old Testament
usage of the word fear as awe and wonder issuing in adoration and praise, the question becomes ours. Do we love
God for God or for what He will do for us? That's the real

question we must ask ourselves in the time when our prayers seem to be unanswered.

But the time when we wonder about unanswered prayer is also God's time to question us. That's what He did to Job. He did not come in a calm, peaceful reassurance of Job's innocence, but in a whirlwind of disturbing questions. "Now prepare yourself like a man; I will question you, and you shall answer Me" (Job 40:7). The Lord faces Job with his arrogant pride which has questioned the purpose, power, and providence of the creator and sustainer of the universe.

Listen to some of the questions the Lord asked Job. "Where were you when I laid the foundations of the earth? Tell Me, if you have understanding. Who determined its measurements? Surely you know! Or who stretched the line upon it? To what were its foundations fastened? Or who laid its cornerstone, when the morning stars sang together, and all the sons of God shouted for joy?" (Job 38:4-7). Throughout the rest of chapters 38–40 the Lord mounts confrontive questions which expose Job's arrogant questioning of the Almighty. Who controls the sea? Who commands the morning and the cycle of day and night? Who sets the length of a person's life? Who gives the rain and snow in season? Who built the mountains? Who created the wonder of conception and birth? Who developed the species of plant, animal, and mammal life? All the questions of God reach a crescendo with the ultimate demand to one who demanded that He be accountable: "Shall the one who contends with the Almighty correct Him? He who rebukes God, let him answer it" (Job 40:2).

At last, in humble submission, Job surrendered his demand that the Lord justify Himself to him. In the last chapter of the book of Job, we witness how the Lord dealt with the sufferer. God answered Job's prayers not with any self-justifying explanation but with His presence. Then Job is able to pray, "I know that You can do everything, and that no purpose of Yours can be withheld from You. You asked, 'Who is this who hides counsel without knowledge?' Therefore I have uttered what I did not understand, things too wonderful for me, which I did not know. Listen, please, and let me speak; you said, 'I will question you, and you shall answer Me.' I have heard of You by the hearing of the ear, but now my eye sees You" (Job 42:2-5).

The question of unanswered prayer is not really our question at all, but the Lord's. What He asked Job, He asks us. "Who is this who hides counsel without knowledge?" Or put another way, "Who is this who withholds answers to our prayers without purpose?" The question forces us to think much more humbly about our audacious questioning of God. But the question also prompts the Lord's penetrating questions, not unlike the ones given to Job but with greater impact. In the context of the incarnation and Pentecost, the Lord reviews not only His creation but also His redemptive acts in Jesus Christ. It is at the foot of the cross, beside an empty tomb, in a Pentecost Upper Room, that He questions us about His readiness to answer prayer. "What more need I do?" And our response is, "Nothing, Lord, just give us your presence and all our questions will melt away!"

Job has taught us three crucial things about our dilemma with unanswered prayer.

All Prayers Are Answered

The first is that *all prayers are answered*. There is a great difference between unanswered prayer and ungranted petitions. Wishing is not real praying. We could have our wants granted and not have received an answer to prayer. The purpose of prayer is communion and con-

The period of waiting for the granting of some requests is often rewarded by a far greater gift than what we asked for. The Lord Himself.

versation with God. The period of waiting for the granting of some request is often rewarded by a far greater gift than what we asked for. The Lord Himself. What is delayed or denied is according to a much greater plan and wisdom than we possess in our finite perception.

A dry spell, when it seems that the Lord has departed from us, is a sure sign that we are on the edge of a new level of depth in our relationship with the Lord. The purpose of unanswered prayer is to lead us from hearsay to heartsight. Job could say, "I have heard of You by the hearing of the ear, but now my eye sees You."

Oswald Chambers said, "Our understanding of God is the answer to prayer. Getting things from God is His indulgence of us. When He stops giving us things, He brings us into the place where we can begin to understand Him. As long as we get from God everything we ask for, we never get to know Him; we look at Him as a blessing machine. Your Father knows what you have need of before you ask Him. Then why pray? To get to know your Father. It is not enough to be able to say 'God is love.' We have to *know* that He is love. We have to struggle through until we do see His love and justice. Then our prayer is answered."[3]

> Thy gifts alone cannot suffice
>   Unless Thyself be given
> Thy presence makes my paradise
>   And where Thou art is heaven.[4]

It is during those periods of what seems to be unanswered prayer that we discover what Paul realized when his pleas for the healing of his "thorn in the flesh" appeared to be unheeded. Many have conjectured about what this physical malady might have been. Suggestions have been made that the apostle suffered malaria, poor eyesight, or energy draining infection. The word "thorn" in Greek really means "stake" which strongly supports the case for malaria which is often attended with excruciating headaches. Perhaps Paul felt like a stake was being driven into his cranium. The point is we do not know. Good thing! Our lack of specific knowledge of the diagnosis enables us to identify with whatever problem, perplexity, or person causes us pain—driving a stake of distress into our hearts. Then we can appreciate what the Lord said to Paul, "My grace is sufficient for you, for My strength is made perfect in weakness" (2 Cor. 12:9).

Like Job, the Apostle Paul had come to a place in his spiritual pilgrimage where he bordered on pride. There is no more debilitating pride than the misuse of prayer as a manipulative device to get what we want when we want it. Prayer becomes a substitute for the Lord Himself. In those times He delays what we think is best for us until we want Him more than an answer according to our specifications.

The personal and practical application to all this is that when prayers seem unanswered, take it as a signal that the Lord wants to help us discover our sufficiency in Him and not what He can give us in tangible blessings.

When I talked with the woman who had written me the note about what seemed to her to be unanswered prayer, I discovered that she was facing physical difficulties and a breakdown of communication in her marriage. She had asked the Lord for healing and a change in her relationship with her husband. The more we talked, the more I became convinced that she needed the Lord more than she needed physical health or the change in her husband's attitudes which she had delegated the Lord to pull off for her. Prior to these difficulties her relationship with the

Lord had drifted into vague blandness. Her physical and relational problems had shocked her into a realization that she needed God's help. But did she need or want God? That was the issue!

I asked a penetrating question. "What if you are not healed and your marriage fails? Will you still want God for God?" That alarmed her and prepared her for some deep conversation about allowing the Lord to be her ultimate and total security—for now and eternity. After several visits she was ready to surrender herself completely to the Lord's love and care. She told Him that she wanted a consistent and abiding relationship with Him more than the answer she had demanded. His Spirit entered her ready mind and heart.

Subsequently, prayers by me and the elders of the church for her physical healing were answered. The stress which had been hindering the flow of the Lord's healing Spirit was dissipated and she could receive what He had been willing to give all along. The woman was also ready to stop blaming her husband for all that was wrong in her marriage, and asked the Lord to change their marriage beginning with her. When she let up on her criticism and complaining, and became the Lord's person in her marriage, her husband was amazed at what was happening to his wife. Because she had surrendered him and his attitudes to the Lord, her efforts to change him were replaced by an effort to be to him the love and forgiveness the Lord was increasingly becoming to her. Eventually, when he could no longer blame his wife for the problems in their marriage, he was motivated to get help with his own attitudes. A Christian counselor put him through the paces of marriage counseling which resulted in a radical personality transformation. Though he had been a member of the church and active in the program, he too had not known the Lord personally. The counselor completed his program of helping him by leading him through a prayer of commitment and a willingness to receive the Holy Spirit as the power to implement what he had discovered about what it meant to love and care for his wife.

What the woman had called an unanswered prayer when she first appealed for help was really not a denial of her prayers but the Lord's wise delay. He did answer, but in so much greater way than she had dared to anticipate. The Lord answered first with Himself, then with spiritual healing of her soul, and finally a solution beyond her expectation.

Not Ready to Receive

This leads us to the second thing the Lord wants to teach us in times in which we feel He has not answered our prayers. The woman I've described asked for help but was not ready to receive what the Lord was willing to give. Now we must consider unanswered prayers for things which *may not be best for us or are not in keeping with the Lord's timing for us.* When I think of some of my "unanswered" prayers, I am filled with thanksgiving and praise! Looking back on some ungranted petitions I am gratified that the Lord said no. If I had received them they would not have been maximum for me or the people around me. Further, some of them were not consistent with the Lord's primary calling for my life. Reflecting on them, if I had received what I asked, I would have drifted into an eddy out of the main stream of His particularized will for me as an individual.

A good example of this in my life has been the way the Lord led me into a national television ministry. Seven years ago I thought I knew exactly what I should do. I devised a format for a program which featured interviews and performances by Christian stars and leaders with a very brief, closing meditation done by me at the end. Three pilot programs were completed featuring people like Jimmy Stewart, Carol Lawrence, and Dale and Roy Rogers. Not a bad billing for success! But efforts to raise money for a full series and syndication seemed blocked at every turn. Even though a large company in America offered to be sponsor, the networks were reluctant to run a "religious" program on prime time. Since the company only wanted a network program, that possibility was lost. Other schemes of syndication were tried with little response. Even those who turned down the program could not explain why.

All the time I was praying and disturbed by what appeared to me to be no answer from the Lord. Finally, I cried out, "What's wrong, Lord? Where have I missed in what I thought was your plan for me?" Silence for weeks. Then one day I received a series of phone calls from trusted friends. One of them articulated clearly the same thought all the others had tried to communicate. "Lloyd," he said, "you've spent all your life allowing the Lord to teach you how to preach the Bible for people's deepest needs. Don't spend time on television interviewing and featuring famous names. Just do what you do best—talk to people about their hopes and hurts and introduce them to the abundant and eternal life in Christ. I was praying about you this morning and aching over your period of unanswered prayer and suddenly I felt a rush of inspiration about your need. It was so strong, I wrote it down. What came to me is what I've just shared with you. I may be off base, but pray about it and see if the Lord confirms it in your own heart and mind."

That phone call led me into an experiment. I gave up the plans of the program I had wanted to do so urgently. I let go of it completely. A few days later, a man in my congregation went to the business manager of my church and gave him a check for a pilot for a very different kind of format. He said the money could be used only if I preached as the main focus of a half-hour format. His specifications perfectly matched the guidance my friend had shared on the phone. I exclaimed with assurance, "Sometimes the Lord gives and takes away, but in this case He took away and gave back—what He wanted all along."

The pilot production confirmed the new direction. Commitment to broadcast portions of the church's worship, including the sermon and music, was affirmed by the Lord in a gift through a will. The woman who had left the money had specifically directed that it should be used for expanding the Pastor's communication of the gospel. It was just enough for the first thirteen weeks' cost of production and airing on a local Los Angeles station.

Now years later, as the program reaches over three hundred cities in America, I look back at the goodness of the Lord in denying one prayer so He could give me a different strategy. When I was willing, He guided me each step of the way in how to talk to the nation about His grace. He showed me how to ask people to share their deepest needs, most urgent questions, and demanding challenges. People responded in hundreds of letters each week. What has resulted is that speaking on the program is like a conversation between friends. I know what people need from their own expressions and can respond with personal messages from the Bible.

This is no easy success story. Each week I face financial needs for the television ministry which press me into deeper trust and dependence on God. And He is faithful in helping me meet obligations through gifts from viewers motivated to help by Him. There's never a dime to spare.

And I must be cautious never to grasp what He has presently led me to do, and demand that He be faithful in only that direction. He may have other plans and a shift in strategy for the future. If so, when it is right in His planning, He will make it clear.

Not Play God

A final thing I want to say about what seems to be unanswered prayer is a word of caution. Like Job's friends, sometimes *we play God in other people's lives by suggesting that all unanswered prayer is caused by some sin in their lives*. This is simplistic and leads to defensive self-incrimination. The result is that people usually blame themselves and seldom seek the Lord Himself as the ultimate answer to all prayer. To be sure, God often delays an answer until He has prepared us to be ready for the blessing He has ready.

Our responsibility is not to accuse people of sin as an explanation of why their prayers seem not to be answered. Rather, if a person suggests that may be the cause we can ask, "Tell me, what do you think may be standing in the way?" If, in response, some sin is confessed, we are to help a person tell God about that and help him or her receive and know His forgiveness. Often that breaks the bind and he or she can be open to the Lord's answer.

The danger comes when we think we can ever be pure enough to deserve God's answers. That leads to pride. What's more, it becomes manipulation of the Almighty. We've all known times when the Lord has helped us when we least deserved it. And we know others whose lives are not spiritually impeccable who are graciously cared for by the Lord. Petulant perfectionism is boldly contradicted by those times when He uses us to help others know or grow

What seems to be unanswered prayer is also a part of His instigation and invitation to communion and conversation with Him on a deeper level. He wants us to know Him more profoundly than ever.

in Him while we still have problems in our own lives. We can empathize with people's needs because we are acutely aware of our own. The result is that we lead people to the Lord and not to ourselves!

So when our prayers seem unanswered, yes, let's ask ourselves if there is a practice, habit, relationship, or misconception which may be blocking the flow of the Lord's Spirit in us. But also, let's never move beyond humble confession to attempts at haughty control. We will never be good enough to earn either salvation or the gifts the Lord longs to give us. If we could be, the cross would not have been necessary.

We are back to our central theme. Prayer starts with God. What seems to be unanswered prayer is also a part of His instigation and invitation to communion and conversation with Him on a deeper level. He wants us to know Him more profoundly than ever. When we feel our prayers are not answered according to our specifications and timing, that feeling is really a longing for God and not just for what He can give or do for us. Thank God for those times. By them we know we have been called into a much more intimate relationship than we've ever known before!

Notes

1. Thomas Hardy, "Impercipient", Gerald DeWitt Sanders and John H. Nelson, eds., *Chief Modern Poets of England and America* (New York: MacMillan Pub. Co., Inc., 1943).
2. Helmut Thielicke, source unknown.
3. Oswald Chambers, source unknown.
4. Source unknown.

For Further Thought . . .

1. Are there times when your prayer life has suddenly become "sterile and unrewarding"? Do you ever become frustrated by what seems to be unanswered prayer? What provision does God make for these moments of frustration?

2. What does our author suggest we do when our prayers seem like they are going unanswered? What does God want us to have even more than answered prayers?

3. What are some of the reasons God may delay His answer to our prayers? Can you apply any of these reasons to your life?

4. Sum up from this chapter what you feel is the most important aspect of prayer.

CHAPTER SEVEN

PRAYER AND HEALING

This past week, I had a power failure in my home and in my life. The first became symbolic of the second. A violent storm cut the power lines which had fed electricity to my neighborhood. We were without electricity for hours. The lights and appliances were totally inoperable.

As I stumbled about in the darkness I was tempted to blame the lamps and light bulbs. That made me think about how absurd it would be to go up to the refrigerator and kick it saying, "You dumb refrigerator, why don't you work!?" It would have been equally unproductive to pound the stove saying, "Why you inefficient, inadequate stove, why don't you do what you were manufactured to do?" In the same way I could not lambaste the air-conditioning system when it did not produce throughout the long, powerless night. A whole section of Los Angeles was without the energy we take for granted with a flick of a switch.

That same week I experienced an overload of the circuits in my spiritual life. I took on too much. My own concerns, worry over people, and a humanly impossible schedule, broke the circuits. So much that I was attempting to get done was only what *I* had determined was crucial. Momentarily I forgot that there's enough time in any one day to do what the Lord wills us to do. Exhaustion set in. While doing a television taping I realized the overload was making me less than maximum. What was usually done with ease became arduous and difficult. Living on my own resources proved to be very inefficient. The business of the previous days had shortened my devotional time and the pressures had distracted me enough so that I didn't draw on the divine energy I usually find so sufficient through moment-by-moment prayer through each responsibility.

In the midst of the spiritual power failure the electricity failure occurred in my home. The parable was so pointed it made me burst out laughing at myself. The feeling of being out of power spiritually had prompted me to fall back into an old pattern of self-incrimination. "Lloyd, what's the matter with you!? You're a producer. You're supposed to pour out work—speaking, writing, pastoring, communicating on television. Now get with it!" Then, as I thought about the inadequacy of the light bulbs, refrigerator, stove and air-conditioning system without electricity, the Lord seemed to say, "My son, you were created to be a transmitter of me. You've blocked the flow of my spirit by attempting more in this week than I guided and set as priorities. You've had a power failure just like your house. To do my will effectively, you must depend on me and the flow of my power."

Ever have a day, week, or period like that? I suspect we all have. You may be experiencing a time of power failure right now as you read this. The solution, as I discovered repeatedly, is not to condemn ourselves but to reestablish the power hookup that profound prayer offers.

The night of the electricity failure I went to bed realizing what the deepest need in my life was. It was not to finish up all my tasks or get from under the burden of pressure. What I needed most of all was to open myself again to the power of the Spirit of the Lord. My prayer time before I went to sleep was a plea for the Lord to take over and do through me what He wanted done. I slept serenely and peacefully. My waking thought was amazing. It was so captivating that I got up and wrote it down. Seven words that helped me know that the power of the Lord was back on in my life: "Nothing has changed, but everything is different!" My desk was still piled high with demanding tasks, the schedule was still full, people's needs still concerned me. But *I* was different. In the flow of the Holy Spirit power I could prioritize, work with freedom, and enjoy being used by the Lord. The power failure was over!

A man shared with me a very moving experience he had in the sanctuary during the worship one Sunday evening. He said, "I had come to the service with a great need for healing in my spiritual and physical life. During the opening prayer I told the Lord how much I needed Him. I felt completely devoid of power. Then as you were finishing up the sermon, I felt a hand on my shoulder. I looked around to see if someone in the pew behind me was touching me or was trying to get my attention. The people behind me smiled but clearly indicated that they had not touched my shoulder. Then it happened again. After that I felt a warmth surge through my body. I felt the hand that had touched my shoulder was now connected to an arm that was joined by another arm to embrace me. I felt loved, accepted, cared about deeply. The Lord was answering the prayer I had prayed about my needs. I felt His Spirit surging through me. The tensions in my mind relaxed, my body felt calm, and my emotions were filled with joy. It was as if an electric current passed through every fibre of my being. Could it be that I received a touch from the Lord?"

It is important to mention that this man is a brilliant intellectual who is not highly emotional or spiritually expressive. He is a down-to-earth, practical, straightforward kind of man. In fact, he is reserved, sometimes very cautious, and genuinely scientific about the way he talks about evidence in any realm. When he went to his doctor the following week, the physical illness from which he had been suffering had radically improved. Subsequently, in the weeks that followed, he was completely healed. This was not in contradiction to the medical aid he was receiving, but a divine intervention which maximized what the medical profession was trying to do to help him. His prayer, "Lord, I desperately need you!" had opened the circuit.

As this man told me what happened, the melody and words of the gospel hymn flooded my mind and heart.

He touched me, O, He touched me,
and O, the joy that floods my soul;
Something happened, and now I know,
He touched me and made me whole.[1]

The Healing Touch

We should not be surprised when God touches a person. I've had it happen often. We should expect it when we gather for worship or are alone in the quiet of our own prayers. We all need the healing touch. The Lord is the source of all healing. When we are in need of healing spiritually, physically, emotionally, interpersonally, or in some problem of life, the Lord knows, cares, and wants to help us. The Church was meant to be a healing community and each of us is called to be an agent of healing. The healing ministry of Jesus Christ manifest so powerfully during the incarnation, is now entrusted to the Church. Prayer is our channel of power to pray for His healing in our own and others' lives. What happened to that man as he sat in church should be anticipated and gratefully expected. In sanctuaries, doctors' offices, operating rooms, hospitals, psychiatrists' counseling rooms, and in research laboratories searching for cures to virulent disease—the divine Healer is at work. He is seeking to release His healing power.

The Healing Power of Prayer

I want to consider with you the healing power of prayer. To do that I want to take James 5:13-16, one of the most incisive passages in the Bible, as a launching pad to consider other passages which deal with Christ's healing power. Before me are the urgent questions we all have about healing. What is spiritual healing? Is the Lord the source of all healing? Why are some we pray for not healed? When a person is not healed according to our timing and specifications, is that an evidence of lack of faith or some hidden sin in their lives? What about the effectiveness of healing ministries in the church or on television? How can we participate in spiritual healing in a biblically intelligent, and Christ-inspired way?

Keeping those questions before us, let's look at James's call to be a healing community. "Is anyone among you suffering? Let him pray. Is anyone cheerful? Let him sing psalms. Is anyone among you sick? Let him call for the elders of the church, and let them pray over him, anointing him with oil in the name of the Lord. And the prayer of faith will save the sick, and the Lord will raise him up. And if he has committed sins, he will be forgiven.

The Lord had called His followers to a ministry of preaching the gospel, teaching His message, and healing the sick. This threefold ministry is ours today also.

Confess your trespasses to one another, and pray for one another, that you may be healed. The effective, fervent prayer of a righteous man avails much" (Jas. 5:13-16).

This was written by James, the Lord Jesus' brother, around 50 A.D. In chapter 1, verse 18, he clarified the special calling of the early Christians, many of whom were facing severe difficulties living out their faith in a hostile secular world. Speaking of the Lord's plan and purpose for the Church, the new creation, he wrote, "Of His own will He brought us forth by the word of truth, that we might be a kind of firstfruits of His creatures." The evidence of the new age of the Messiah is the Messiah's people. As we said in the previous chapter, He seeks to do through us what He did in the incarnation. For James, a vital dimension of the Lord's continuing ministry through His people is healing of the manifold needs of people. The Lord had called His followers to a ministry of preaching the gospel, teaching His message, and healing the sick. This threefold ministry is ours today also.

The Meaning of Healing

To claim that, we need to understand what healing is in its full biblical meaning. James uses two very basic words for healing in this passage. In 5:15 he says that the prayer of faith will "save" the sick. This is the future active of the Greek word *sōzō*, to make well or whole. It also is a key New Testament word for salvation and wholeness as well as healing. In verse 16, "that you may be healed" the first aorist past subjunctive of *iaomai* was used in the New Testament for healing of both body and the soul.

The word *sōzō* is used for salvation and healing in Jesus' message and in the epistles. The noun form is *sōtēria* and it means "deliverance from danger, suffering, sin, and sickness" and was the primary word to describe the eternal salvation given to those who believed in Jesus Christ as Lord and Saviour (see Acts 2:47). In Jesus' assertion of why He came, He said, "For God did not send His Son into the world to condemn the world, but that the world through Him might be saved" (John 3:17). Again the word *sōzō* is used for His Aramaic word for "save." He came to deliver us from evil, sin, sickness, and death, but also to heal the whole person. He was concerned about our abundant life and eternal life. The Saviour's *(Sōtēr)* life, death, and resurrection was for our salvation *(sōtēria)* and the healing of all our brokenness spiritually and emotionally *(sōzō)*. Christ offered a salvation that encompassed the whole person. That's why He healed the sick as a sign that God was in Him to heal bodies, minds, and relationships as well as to suffer for the sins of the world on the cross.

The Source of Healing

There is one and only one source of healing. The Creator, Sustainer, and Redeemer of all creation is healing. This healing power dwelt incarnate in Jesus. When He touched the sick, deranged, or troubled, they were healed. The blind received sight, the lame walked, and the mentally disturbed were liberated.

After Pentecost, the Lord gave spiritual gifts to His followers for the healing of the varied needs of people. Paul lists these in 1 Corinthians 12. Particularly crucial were the gifts of faith, healing, and working of miracles. They equipped the Christians to dare to believe in the Lord's power to heal, actually pray for healing, and see miracles result.

The same healing power which had been revealed in the incarnation was unleashed through the early Christians. It happened just as Jesus promised. The early Church preached a salvation which included atonement for sin, reconciliation with God, and healing of the sick. Like their Master, the daring believers had a view of salvation that was inclusive of the whole person—physically, emotionally, and spiritually. There was no idea that the Lord only saved a soul for heaven and cared little for the body in which that soul lived. That came later in the Middle Ages when salvation was focused primarily on the soul and its future salvation in heaven. It is interesting to note that the anointing with oil for the healing of the sick was changed into the sacrament of extreme unction at the time of death.

The Healing Ministry of the Church

Today we have widely divergent views of the healing ministry of the Church. There are some who are convinced that the role of the Church is to preach eternal salvation and that the care of the physical needs of people is the exclusive responsibility of the medical profession. Others preach salvation but make a major emphasis on the healing ministry. Still others emphasize healing by prayer alone and deny the use of medicine or consultation of the medical profession.

I hold what I believe is a biblical view that we are to minister to the whole person—body, mind, soul, as well as everything which concerns a person's interpersonal and social needs. We are to lead people to Christ, introduce them to the abundant life in Him, expose the secret of power in His indwelling Spirit, and help them grow in Him in every area of life. Our calling is to affirm all means of healing of the mind and body. This involves support of the medical professions and cooperative efforts to minister to the whole person.

But in addition to that, I am convinced that we are called to a specific prayer ministry for the manifold ill-

Members and friends of our congregations need an opportunity to bring their varied needs for specific prayer.

nesses and maladies of people. This should include prayer with individuals at times of sickness, prayer groups for intercession for the sick, and public services for prayer for the spiritual, emotional, and physical needs of people. Members and friends of our congregations need an opportunity to bring their varied needs for specific prayer.

James provides guidelines for this ministry of healing. Note the many kinds of needs enumerated in the passage we cited earlier. There were those who were suffering who needed to pray. Others were cheerful and needed to give thanks by singing psalms to avoid pride and self-sufficiency. Then there were the sick who needed prayer for healing and anointing with oil signifying the blessing of the Spirit of the Lord. But there were also those who had fallen into sin and were in need of forgiveness.

In any congregation gathered for worship all these needs and others suggested by these categories are present in our people. There are those whose deepest need is to receive Christ as Saviour and Lord of their lives. Others are facing problems in living the Christian life that need to be committed to the Lord. Still others have broken relationships which need reconciliation. Some have committed sins or known deep failure who need forgiveness and assurance of pardon. And then there are those who are distressed emotionally or under the grip of psychological problems. Finally, there are people who are ill, facing crippling diseases, grim prognoses, and debilitating physical pain. If we really care about people, some way must be devised to give individual and specific attention to these varied dis-eases and dis-tresses. A healing ministry is essential to bring people into contact and communion with the Great Physician.

In my church in Hollywood, we have followed James's admonition. The elders of the church have taken the biblical injunction seriously. They are not only the lay leaders of the spiritual life of the church and administrators of the program of the congregation, but they have been ordained to be channels of healing power through prayer for the manifold needs of the people. This is done periodically when a major portion of the Sunday morning service is set aside for prayers for the spectrum of physical, emotional, spiritual and relational problems people are suffering. After the morning message, they gather on the chancel steps to pray with people who come forward from the congregation. After sharing their specific need they are asked to kneel and the elder lays hands on them and prays for the release of the Lord's healing power in them. People come forward seeking to know Christ, others need assurance of forgiveness, some have concerns for loved ones who are ill or troubled. Many have physical illness and still others are facing challenges where they need the Lord's guidance and strength. The results of these prayers have been astounding.

So often in worship, the preaching, prayers, and music skim over the inner needs of people. The ministry of prayer for healing of the whole person gives an opportunity for people to respond to the Spirit and receive personal help.

Since it would be difficult to take a fifteen-minute section of every Sunday's worship for a healing service, we set aside specific Sundays throughout the year for this. But, because needs cannot be scheduled according to a church worship calendar, the elders come forward every Sunday during the singing of the concluding hymn. During that time and after the service they pray for individuals who have responded to the invitation to receive Christ or ask for prayer for a specific physical or spiritual problem. So the healing ministry, emphasized periodically with a special service, also takes place every Sunday at the conclusion of the weekly services.

The elders are not the only people who pray for the diversity of needs. Hundreds of members of the congregation have responded to the call to a ministry of intercession. A list of the needs of people is distributed weekly to those people for daily prayers. Sensitized by the emphasis of healing prayer throughout the life of the Church, people pray for one another one to one, in small prayer groups, and over the phone. The power of God is being released through His people! The Holy Spirit gift of healing is being claimed and exercised. No one elevates himself or herself to a permanent status of being a "healer." Rather the need presented by one brings forth the gift of healing in another.

The reason that the shared ministry of healing is so crucial is that at times of need often we are unable to pray for ourselves creatively. Problems, frustrations, and physical or emotional illness debilitates our capacity to hope and pray boldly for ourselves. That's when we desperately need to be able to share our disability with a sensitive, empathetic friend who believes that the Lord is able and all that He wills is possible.

When There Is No Healing

At this point in our consideration of prayer and healing we must face some of the hard questions we raised earlier. What about those for whom we pray and they do not get well? The temptation is to blame ourselves, our effectiveness in prayer, or the other person for resisting the healing. So often people say, "If I would have had more faith, my prayers would have been answered!" Or we subtly suggest that the person being prayed for does not have adequate faith or has some hidden sin or unconfessed rebellion against the Lord.

Surely there are times when we pray faithless prayers. And we've all known periods when we blocked the Spirit's way in us. Also we've observed those spiritual impediments in others. James confronts the problem head-on. "Confess your trespasses to one another, and pray for one another, that you may be healed" (Jas. 5:16). Note carefully that he did not say, "Your sickness is caused by sin. Therefore confess your sins to one another alarming each other with the danger of unconfessed sin." Helping another person honestly face anything which might debilitate healing must be done with tenderness and sensitivity. There are times when, after patient listening to another person share the area of need for prayer, I am led to ask one or both of these questions: "How do you feel about your need?" or "Now, before we pray, is there anything you know of that may be standing in the way of God's Spirit in your life?" I never ask either question without sharing my own answers in times of need in my life. In answer to the first question I share times when I have felt impatience, fear, or disappointment and longed for the Lord to intervene. I relate how I grew as a person in those times and how the Lord's answers were eventually given when the time was right. In response to the second question I can talk about times in the past when resentments, unhealed relationships, or unwillingness to act on guidance the Lord has given, kept me unwilling to receive what the Lord has offered to heal a problem or sickness. That usually primes the pump of honest sharing from a person for whom I am about to pray. Sometimes their response is "I don't know of anything." I take them at their word and proceed with the prayer for their need.

In our prayers for the sick, not all get well. The danger is that we think that either God did not hear us or that we didn't pray hard enough. The ministry of praying for others is often judged by our successes or failures. That's to play God. Or we stop praying for others because we didn't get what we thought was best when we thought it should happen. Our task is to be faithful and leave the results to God. His timing is perfect and His answers often come in ways we did not expect.

For example, I prayed for a man who was very ill. There seemed to be no physical change for months other than he felt the comfort of trusting God completely with his need. During the long illness, he came to know the Lord more intimately than ever before. He developed a closer relationship with his family and expressed love more profoundly than he had previously. Through this, his wife became a Christian and his joy in suffering was a moving witness to friends and fellow workers. Then the combination of prayer and the skill of a Christ-guided physician restored him to health. The Lord had timed the recovery perfectly. So much more than the man's body had been healed.

What About Death?

But what about death? Have we failed in our prayers for healing if someone dies? Not if we believe that death for a Christian is only a transition in eternal life. Again we must trust the Lord. He has conquered over the power of death. We are alive forever when we belong to Christ. Of course we feel grief, that's an honest expression of a physical loss. But for a person in Christ, death is not a tragedy but a triumph. Heaven is the unlimited, maximized union with the Lord, and the unfettered experience of the love, joy, and peace of which we have realized in part during the years of life in the physical body.

Once we get free of judging the Lord for the results of

our prayers we are liberated to pray boldly and leave the outcome to Him.

A surgeon friend of mine confessed that the most difficult transition he passed through in his healing ministry through surgery was when he realized that remorse over those who did not get well was not going to keep him from excellence in doing his best with God's help in his care for people. He said he made a covenant with the Lord to be the finest surgeon he could be, pray through each surgery, and claim God's healing power. "I decided that I was not going to brood over losing one patient and become ineffective in caring for hundreds of others." The same is true for all of us in our intercessory prayers for the healing of the needs of others. The Lord is in charge; our task is to become cooperative prayer partners in His healing.

We have come full circle to where we began. An awesome trust has been given to us to pray for healing. The power to do that is the Lord's and not ours. Our responsibility is to keep the power lines open. When we overload or blow the circuits by running our own lives, we become ineffective transmitters of hope and courage to others. We live in a sick and suffering world. The gift of healing is offered to us for our prayers for people and their needs. Keeping the power lines open will make all the difference to the people whom the Lord will put on our agenda to pray for healing. James was right: "The effective, fervent prayer of a righteous man avails much." And that effectiveness and fervency comes from the Lord. He has made us right with Himself because He has decided to use human agents like us to accomplish His healing in the bodies, minds and spirits of His people.

For Further Thought . . .

1. When was the last time your spiritual circuit experienced an overload? What elements made up this situation? Did you find yourself feeling exhausted? discouraged? angry? depressed? Describe your feelings.

2. What does God offer us in times of overload and power failure?

3. What is the channel of power God gives each of us for the healing of ourselves and others? What part do we play in someone's physical or spiritual healing?

4. Several early Church needs were listed in this chapter. Do those same needs exist today? List the needs you ought to be praying for.

CHAPTER EIGHT

THE NAME THAT CHARMS OUR FEARS

Just before I gave a prayer at a civic gathering, the chairman of the meeting said, "Lloyd, I hope you won't end your prayer in Jesus' name. This is a mixed gathering with several different religions represented and I wouldn't want anyone to be offended."

How would you have reacted to that? Would you have left out Jesus' name as you ended your prayer? If so, would the prayer have been less effective? What do you think about when you end a prayer in the Lord's name? Is that simply a rote habit or does it make any difference in the content and power of the prayer?

When I ended my prayer that day at the civic meeting, I said, "In the name that is above every name, Yahweh, and the one who was highly exalted and given that name, even Jesus Christ. Amen." When I returned to my seat the chairman was pleased. He thought I had followed instructions. That led to a deep conversation about why I had ended the way I did. Actually, what I had said was much stronger. After the meeting, we visited late into the evening about Jesus Christ and how to pray in His name. I was glad that I had held fast to my convictions.

Jesus told us to pray in His name. "Most assuredly, I

say to you, he who believes in Me, the works that I do he will do also; and greater works than these he will do, because I go to My Father. And whatever you ask in My name, that I will do, that the Father may be glorified in the Son. If you ask anything in My name, I will do it" (John 14:12-14).

That tells us several crucial things for praying with power. We are promised that we will be given authority to do what Jesus did. That means that the same power to love, forgive, heal, reconcile, and live out the kingdom of God we witness in Jesus' life and ministry can be done by us. Further, it tells us that Jesus wants to continue His ministry through us. Note that He forcefully claims that He will be the implementing agent. "I will do it" assures us that the risen Christ, glorified and reigning through the power of the Spirit, will undertake to accomplish prayers prayed in His name.

Jesus spoke that promise in the context of the Hebrew reverence for the power of the name. In Hebrew "the name" was synonymous with God. It was used for the character, authority, and power of God. The one name which no Hebrew ever spoke audibly was Yahweh. It was considered so sacred that the word *Adonai* was used. The name Yahweh was the name given Moses at the burning bush. I AM WHO I AM God told him. The phrase is the Hebrew causative verb "to be." It means "I will make happen." The new name given Moses by God was HAYAH, rendered YHWH, or Yahweh, the Lord. When Jesus said I AM in twenty-three crucial statements in His ministry, He was boldly claiming to be none other than Yahweh, God present in the Immanuel. Prayer in His name is able to unleash the power of God. Jesus Christ is the wisdom and power of God with us.

Now look at what Paul said about Christ in Philippians

2. We are told that we can expect to have the mind of Christ (v. 5). Then the apostle tells us whose mind it is that we can receive in our prayers. He tells us about the humiliation, obedience, and exaltation of Christ. Then he says an astounding thing. "Therefore God also has highly exalted Him and given Him the name which is above every name, that at the name of Jesus every knee should bow, of those in heaven, and of those on earth, and of those under the earth, and that every tongue should confess that Jesus Christ is Lord, to the glory of God the Father" (vv. 9-11). What is the name that is above every name? Jesus? Hardly. Though the name meant "Jehovah is salvation," there were many, both during and after Jesus of Nazareth, with that name. Christ? No, because that would put the name of "Anointed One," *Messiah,* above the name of God. There is only one name that is above every other name. *Yahweh!* The very name Jesus used when He boldly claimed that He was the light of the world, the resurrection and the life, and the way the truth and the life—plus all the other I AM assertions. Jesus the Christ is glorified to continue doing what He began in the incarnation, to impart the power of the essential verb, verve, and vitality of God. He is the Logos through whom all things were created and the living Word who recreated us through the atonement. Now as our living Lord, He is Yahweh with us to continue His re-creation in and through you and me.

Therefore Jesus' name is Yahweh. That's what is really meant by the words "in Jesus' name" or more accurately, "In the name given to Jesus, a name above every name, Yahweh." The God who makes things happen is with us and in us to make them continue to happen.

Pray in Keeping with What He Revealed
To pray in Jesus' name of Yahweh implies three things.

The first is to *pray in keeping with what He revealed in His life*, message, death, resurrection, and return in the Holy Spirit at Pentecost. We can be sure that the Lord will not contradict His message. Anything which denies His atoning death and perpetrates our self-justification will not be answered. He told us that we were to seek first the kingdom of God and His righteousness and to pray boldly in keeping with that sublime purpose.

Remember that "the name" represented the character of the one designated. The Lord wants to guide us in asking for that which is in keeping with His character and will further impute His character in us. The more we know of the Lord as revealed in Scripture and deepened in fellowship with Him, the more our prayers will express His will for us. Again we must stress the importance of listening as the major responsibility of prayer. Then we can test any request with this five-fold qualification: (1) Has what I am asking for been refined in meditative, creative listening? (2) If I received the request, would it enable me to grow closer to the Lord? (3) Does it seek the ultimate good of all involved? (4) Will it extend the kingdom of God, His reign and rule in my life and others'? (5) Is it something I can ask the Lord to enjoy with me if He grants it?

Pray in His Power

The second thing praying in Jesus' name, Yahweh, Lord, implies is that *it is accomplished in His power*. Ending a prayer in His name is not a perfunctory addendum. It is asking for the release of supernatural power for the fulfillment of what He has guided us to pray. He wants to continue His ministry through us as He promised. So often we pray for things we could do without His help. He wants us to dare to pray adventuresome prayers only He could accomplish. We are not meant to use prayer as a desire to

When we pray in Jesus' name of Lord we call on the same power He revealed, the same divine energy that raised Him from the dead, and the same Spirit who entered the 20 waiting followers of Jesus in the Upper Room at Pentecost.

get help to do our plan, but power to attempt His plans for us. What in your life could be done only through a supernatural intervention by the living Lord in you? Pray for that!

The power of Jesus Christ the Lord is offered us for the accomplishment of His will as He reveals it to us and for the confrontation of evil. We must consider both.

After the resurrection, Jesus promised that the disciples would be "endued with power from on high" (Luke 24:49). The word for "endued" in Greek is *endusēsthe* from the verb *endunō,* meaning clothed or to put on a garment. This would be done to the followers of Jesus. They were to wait in Jerusalem until it happened. We are reminded of the deeper implications of the Hebrew in the description of what happened to Gideon. "The Spirit of the Lord came upon Gideon; then he blew the trumpet" (Judg. 6:34). The words *come upon* really mean that the Lord clothed Himself with Gideon. This gave Gideon the courage to blow the trumpet and rally the forces of Israel against Midian and dare to go into battle in spite of impossible numerical odds. The image of the Lord entering a frightened man and actually clothing Himself with him is vivid and impelling. What happened through Gideon, and later through the disciples when they were endued—clothed—is exactly what we need when we pray for the challenges the Lord has given us. His work can be done only with His power. Our work done with our strength is humanism. The Lord's work attempted on our strength is religion. But the Lord's work done by His power is the abundant life.

When we pray in Jesus' name of Lord we call on the same power He revealed, the same divine energy that raised Him from the dead, and the same Spirit who entered the 120 waiting followers of Jesus in the Upper

Room at Pentecost. Jesus had promised exactly what happened, "If anyone thirsts, let him come to Me and drink. He who believes in Me, as the Scripture has said, out of his heart will flow rivers of living water" (John 7:37-38). John's comment on this in verse 39 is very pointed. "But this He spoke concerning the Spirit, whom those believing in Him would receive; for the Holy Spirit was not yet given, because Jesus was not yet glorified." The Lord's glorification took place when He ascended, having completed the incarnation, atonement, and resurrection. After His glorification He returned in the power of the Holy Spirit. He "clothed" Himself with His followers, indwelt them so that rivers of His power flowed from them, and they prayed and acted with divine strength beyond their human capacities. The same enduing and engendering is available to us as we pray.

Paul's prayer for the Ephesians reveals what is available to us. He prayed that, according to the riches of the Lord's glory, they would "be strengthened with might through His Spirit in the inner man, that Christ may dwell in your hearts by faith; that you, being rooted and grounded in love, may be able to comprehend with all the saints what is the width and length and depth and height— to know the love of Christ which passes knowledge; that you may be filled with all the fullness of God. Now to Him who is able to do exceedingly abundantly above all that we ask or think, according to the power that works in us . . . " (Eph. 3:16-20). There's a charter for powerful praying. The Lord lives His life in us to guide our prayers beyond what we would dare to ask or think possible. Prayer in His name is prayer by His leading and accomplished by His power. And He does exceedingly abundantly, far more, than we in our human reservations would imagine possible.

But that's not all. The power of Jesus' name enables us to confront and win over the evil powers in the world. Ephesians 6:11-12 in *Phillips* translation makes this very clear. "I expect you have learned by now that our fight is not against any physical enemy, it is against organizations and powers that are spiritual. We are up against the unseen power that controls this dark world, and spiritual agents from the very headquarters of evil." When we pray in Jesus' name we are armed with the one weapon that can defeat satanic influence in our lives and the people for whom we pray. Christ won the battle with Satan when He conquered through the blood of the cross. The Lord of Calvary is our power over Satan's diabolical invasion of situations and people. When we claim the power of the blood of the cross, we can command Satan to take his hands off the Lord's property. The one name he cannot resist is the name of Jesus Christ, the Lord, Yahweh. When our lives become hassled by evil influences we can boldly say, "In the name of Jesus Christ the Lord, leave this situation, person, or group." We do not need to be helpless victims of satanic influence. And further, when we give our lives to Christ and are filled with His Spirit we are sealed against the possibility of possession by Satan's negative, destructive, debilitating power. Persistent prayer in Jesus' name brings His authority and victorious presence that casts out Satan.

Prayer Overcomes Our Fears

That leads us to the third blessing of praying in Jesus' name. *It overcomes our fear.* We all have fears which rob us of the joy of living. We fear certain people, failure, pain, and inadequacy. Beneath all our fears is the fear of losing control and the ability to cope. At the root of this fear is the fear of dying.

Charles Wesley wrote beautifully about the power of the name to overcome our fears. "Jesus! the name that charms our fears, that bids our sorrows cease, 'tis music in the sinner's ears, 'tis life and health and peace."

How does Jesus Christ charm our fears? From my own personal experience He does it in several ways. First, He exposes them for what they are. He helps us ask, "Of what or whom am I afraid?" Then the Lord forces us to face the fear with a further question, "Does this person or situation have any power greater than Christ?" And then He lovingly asks, "Will you give me that fear and allow me to give you courage to overcome it?"

Fear is the outward manifestation of the feeling of insufficiency. We are afraid when we are unsure that we will have what it takes to live, face troubles, endure sickness, and die with assurance of eternal life. We worry over money because of previous shortages. We are troubled by certain kinds of people because of prior hurts by similar personality types. Failures in the past make us catatonic because we fear further failure.

Most of all fear is entangled with what has happened to us in the past. We need a healing of the memories in order to face the future unafraid. The secret of how the Lord does that is given us by the Apostle John. "There is no fear in love; but perfect love casts out fear, because fear involves torment. But he who fears has not been made perfect in love. We love Him because He first loved us" (1 John 4:18-19).

Remember that the one who wrote these words had faced persecution, imprisonment, and constant danger. The remedial remedy for fear he gives us is one he had experienced through long years of communion with the living Lord. He had been the beloved disciple of the Lord, had depended on His love in excruciating circumstances,

and had found Him triumphantly adequate in his trials.
Most of all, he had seen and heard Him say, "Do not be
afraid; I am the First and the Last. I am He who lives, and
was dead, and behold, I am alive forevermore. Amen. And
I have the keys of Hades and of Death" (Rev. 1:17-18).
Note the strong I AM, spoken with the authority of Yahweh. He is the beginning and end of all things. He has conquered death and overcome the forces of evil. John found
that consistent oneness with the Lord cast out his fears.
His love in each potential fear displaced the fear.

Fear can best be defined as the absence of love. The
same emotional channel through which fear is felt and
expressed is also the channel of experiencing and communicating love. The conquest of our fears happens through a
love relationship with our Lord. The more we allow Him to
love us, the more free we will be of fear. Fear is feeling
unloved or being anxious about the consistency and faithfulness of people's love. Christ's love for us is unchanging,
unlimited, and unqualified. He, divine love, fills us with His
Spirit and fear is displaced. Anytime we feel afraid, it is a
sure sign we need to surrender the memory, circumstance, person, or danger to the Lord.

But the ultimate conquest of fear happens when we
accept that nothing or no one can ultimately hurt us. We
are alive forever. Our destiny is sure. And anything in
between now and heaven will be used by the Lord to help
us trust Him more fully. We are indestructible! The Lord
has taken up residence in us and our true inner person will
reign with Him now and through all of eternity. That's the
source of true courage for all of life's battles.

The name of Jesus is more than a title or descriptive
designation of His nature. The name is really sacramental
in that it is an outward sign of a limitless power, authority,
and presence. The word "sacrament" comes from the

*The faithful prayer in the
name of the Lord brings the
effluence of His Spirit, His
wisdom for our decisions, His
strength for our weaknesses,
and His love for our fears.*

Latin *sacramentum,* a mystery. But it also was used for an oath or pledge of allegiance and obedience to Caesar by a Roman legionnaire. Ranking officers of the Roman armies carried a medallion of Caesar's authority. The idea conveyed was that wherever that officer went he could depend on all the authority and power of Rome to be marshalled in any conflict or battle. He had made his oath of obedience to Caesar and knew that the empire's power was available to be called forth.

His Name Gives Us Assurance

In a much more propitious way the name of Jesus Christ, the Lord, gives us greater assurance. Through His name, mysteriously the power of God is released for our needs, complexities, and fears. We are not alone. Our sacred symbol is the cross. The same victorious power revealed there and vindicated in the resurrection is ours. The faithful prayer in the name of the Lord brings the effluence of His Spirit, His wisdom for our decisions, His strength for our weaknesses, and His love for our fears. And in addition to that, He goes before us to invade our difficulties. He deals with people long before we meet them, and unravels problems long before we confront them. Our Lord is able!

The name of the Lord guides our prayers, gives power to implement the answers we are given, and makes us unafraid as we face the future. To pray without the name of the Lord is like trying to sail in a turbulent sea without ever hoisting the main sail to catch the wind. The wind of the Holy Spirit, the present, powerful Christ is available. Hoist the sail, open your heart, and allow Him to enable you to do what He's guided you to pray boldly.

Jesus said, "The things which are impossible with men are possible with God" (Luke 18:27). And the secret of releasing those possibilities is the name above every name, Yahweh. And His presence with us is One who has the authority to bring our impossibilities and His power together. In the light of that I don't want just to end my prayers with The Name, but begin, punctuate, and complete them in the fullness of all He promised He would do through us.

For Further Thought . . .

1. What promise does God give us in John 14:12? What works will we be given authority to do? Under what power will we be able to carry on the ministry of Jesus?

2. What is the name above every name? What does that name mean?

3. How does our author explain the difference between humanism, religion and abundant life?

4. Are you convinced that as a Christian you do not need to be a "helpless victim of satanic influence"? List ways in which our author supports this claim.

CHAPTER NINE

PRAYER IN THE
VALLEY OF DECISION

A friend of mine called to arrange a visit over lunch. "I really need to talk with you," he said urgently. "I've got to make a crucial decision about a job offer I have. It could be the most important career decision of my life. My need is for an objective person to listen and tell me how to make a right decision." I told him I'd be happy to listen and share what I'd learned over the years about discovering God's specific will for particular decisions.

When we got together I quickly discovered that the young executive was very serious about wanting to know God's will for the important decision he had to make. He opened the conversation in earnest. "I don't want to make a wrong choice," he said. "But how do I know for sure what is God's will? I really want to take this job, but what if that's just my will and not the Lord's will for me?"

I replied with some questions. "Can you think of any reason the Lord would not want you to make this a yes decision? Will you be asked to do anything contrary to what you believe? Can you continue to put the Lord first in your life if you take this job? Will this opportunity bring you closer to your life goals professionally? Will it give you a chance to witness for your faith? Can you claim the Lord's presence and power as you do your work?"

He could answer all the questions affirmatively. "When do you have to give an answer to the offer?" I asked. He told me he had a few days. Then I suggested an exercise in prayer that has worked for me in making decisions. "It sounds like you really want to take this job. Why not try that on for the days between now and when you must respond. Live with a 'yes' decision. Ask the Lord to create a conviction of rightness or wrongness. Open yourself in prayer. Yield your mind to Him, surrender your will specifically for this, and ask Him to use everything—circumstances, people you trust, and the Scriptures—to affirm or negate your decision."

A few days later the man called me to tell me that he felt guided to take the job. "I was so concerned," he said. "I thought that because I wanted this, God was probably against it. I couldn't imagine that He would be for me in this!" I reminded him that the Lord was his friend and wanted what was best for him. He had guided the whole process. Because the man was open to allow the Lord to condition his thoughts, he had been given clear direction. In this case all signals were "go!"

Decisions, decisions. We all face them every day. Some are insignificant; others are crucial for our future. In all of them we want to make guided choices. We long to know and do the Lord's will.

The prophet Joel speaks of the valley of decision. "Multitudes, multitudes in the valley of decision!" (Joel 3:14). Times of making crucial decisions force us into that valley. The alternatives force us to make hard choices.

We Are Not Alone

We are not alone in that valley of decision. The Lord is there with us. His ultimate will for us is that we should

God is the initiator of prayer and is the prime mover in the revelation of His will for us. Why would He go to the extents He has to love, forgive, reconcile, and empower us to be His persons, and then leave us without help in making decisions that will shape our destiny?

know, love, glorify, and serve Him. He wills both abundant life and eternal life for us. Both salvation and sanctification are parts of His primary will. And within that awesome context, the Lord also has a personal will for each of us which is His plan for us—unique, particular, and specific.

That does not mean that the Lord's will is a rigid, inflexible set of sealed orders. Rather, the Lord has goals for us, work for us to do, challenges to tackle with His power. Our question is, How do we discover what He wants in each decision?

In every vital decision there is something the Lord does and then something He asks us to do. Let's consider both. The Lord really cares about us. He will not leave us in a quandary when the decisions we face will determine our effectiveness as persons or affect our relationship with Him.

What the Lord Does

Here's what the Lord does to help us in our decisions. Two specific promises from Scripture give us assurance. In Philippians 2:12-13 Paul tells us, "Work out your own salvation with fear and trembling; for it is God who works in you both to will and to do for His good pleasure." This promise refocuses our central theme: God is the initiator of prayer and is the prime mover in the revelation of His will for us. Why would He go to the extents He has to love, forgive, reconcile, and empower us to be His persons, and then leave us without help in making decisions that will shape our destiny? When Paul suggests that we are to work out our own salvation with fear and trembling, he is not suggesting that we can save ourselves by our own self-justification or righteousness. What he is saying, it seems to me, is that we are to live out our salvation in all of life with deep concern that all which we decide and do enables us to grow in that salvation and express its power in all aspects of our life. And the Lord doesn't leave us on our own to do that. He loves us so much that prior, during, and after the major decisions of our lives, He takes the responsibility to work in us a clear conviction of what we are to live out.

He Liberates Our Wills

In the consistent communion of prayer, the Lord works to liberate our wills. The will is the implementor of thought and desire. Thus the Lord's task in us is to clarify His will, condition our thought around His ultimate and specific desires for us so that our wills can function properly with the right goals and plans. The wonder of it all is that He can and will enable us to desire what He desires for us. He gives us an eager mind, desirous of discovering His strategy for our lives. Our thoughts are purified by prolonged and repeated times of prayer. We become expectantly alert to the implanting of the Lord's long- and short-range goals for us. These give us the beginning basis for discerning His will in specific decisions. Added to that, the Lord uses all our faculties to create an assurance of the best choice.

So often we feel we are solely responsible for our decisions. When a big one comes along we think that we should check in with the Lord to get help. Then soon we forget our need of His continuing guidance and live on our own ability. That's to miss the hourly and daily direction He offers.

The Lord knows the future. He foresees the decisions that are ahead of us. The essence of the promise Paul made the Philippians is that, long before the decision must be made, He begins His preparation in us. He uses everything in and around us to condition our thoughts and will in anticipation. The habitual communion of prayer and Bible study gives us the convictions, ideas, and values which will affect our understanding at the time of the decision. Repeated relinquishment of our will makes us ready and receptive. As a result, our wills will not be an impediment, but an implementor of the clarified direction when the decision must be made.

The question I'm asked most often is, How can I know the will of God? The question exposes people's inconsistent communion with the Lord. My answer is not to give people a set of rules to finding God's will but to explain His promise to work in us constantly so that we are ready for the choices of life. That leads to the discipline of prayer, not just for crises, but in daily times of listening and constant communion through the day. That's often more than people bargain for who raise the question about how to know God's will.

Over the years, I have discovered that the Lord does not distribute cheap grace and guidance. He created us for a consistent companionship and redeemed us to live in close oneness with Him. Those who rush to Him only when a decision demands His help are often made to wait. He uses the time of indecision to draw us closer to Him and establish a profound relationship which will prepare us for decisions in the future.

I have a friend who calls her doctor only when she has an illness. She talks to him on the phone and wants a prescription of some miracle drug for whatever malady she has. Consistently, she has resisted general checkups and the doctor's desire to help her with an overall plan of diet, exercise, and health care which would avert her repeated illnesses. Recently he refused to give quickie remedies on the phone and told her she must submit to his comprehensive program of remedial care for her long-range well-being. That would necessitate more than a phone call in crises. The doctor cared too much for this woman's health to continue as a telephone prescription service. How much more the Lord wants to maximize our spiritual lives. He is up to momentous things with us. In His master plan for the kingdom in our time, He has plans for each of us which fit into His overall will. The people around us, the churches of which we are a part, the places we work, and the communities in which we live are dependent on our seeking the Lord's will consistently so that His maximum in every area can be accomplished. When we are out of touch with Him, we make wrong choices, develop unguided programs, and head in directions that are less than He envisions for us. We and others, as well as situations in which we are involved, are cheated.

Hebrews 13:20-21 sounds a trumpet call giving the same promise as the Philippian verses we quoted a few pages back. "Now may the God of peace who brought up our Lord Jesus from the dead, that great Shepherd of the sheep, through the blood of the everlasting covenant, make you complete in every good work to do His will, working in you what is well pleasing in His sight, through Jesus Christ, to whom be glory forever and ever."

The continuing ministry of Christ, God with us, is the focus of this triumphant benediction. Through Him we are participants of the new covenant in His blood. A covenant is a promise. We are covenant members of the new Israel through Christ. Our relationship is based on the grace offered us through the cross. The Lord has called us to be His people and will not let us go. As He took responsibility for our redemption, He assumes the initiative role in "making us complete." The word for "complete" in this stirring passage is *katatisai*, from *katartizō*, meaning "to equip." The Lord equips us to do His will. As indwelling

He readily responds to our willingness and makes His will known for each situation, choice, and decision. To do that He equips us with the gifts of wisdom, knowledge, discernment, and vision.

Lord living in us He gives us whatever we need to know and do His will. He wants us to do what is "well pleasing in His sight." But He does not leave that for us to flounder about until we happen on it. He readily responds to our willingness and makes His will known for each situation, choice, and decision. To do that He equips us with the gifts of wisdom, knowledge, discernment, and vision.

What Is Our Part?

Now, in response to these awesome promises we must consider what our part is in discovering and doing the Lord's will in our decisions. There are three gifts we have to give: An open mind, a responsive will, and a faithful obedience.

An Open Mind

Prayer is the time in which what the Lord has been "working in us" is worked out in clarified thought. *An open mind is attentive.* What He has been developing in our thoughts about His specific guidance is crystalized. When we wait quietly in His presence, the Lord will reform our thinking around His plans for us. William Barclay said, "Here is something to ponder. We are so apt to think that prayer is asking God for what we want, whereas true prayer is asking God for what He wants. Prayer is not only talking to God, even more it is listening to Him."[1]

I find it helpful to say to the Lord, "I consciously yield my capacity to think, which you gave me to guide me in thinking your thoughts." That keeps me from falsely using prayer as a means of persuading God to do what I want. True prayer is intelligent, purposeful conversation with God in which our thinking is reoriented and redirected.

My good friend Paul Rees puts it this way. "If we are willing to take hours on end to learn to play the piano, or operate a computer, or fly an airplane, it is sheer nonsense for us to imagine that we can learn the high art of getting guidance through communion with the Lord without being willing to set time aside for it. It is no accident that the Bible speaks of prayer as a form of waiting on God."[2] But it is not waiting for God to hear, but waiting until our minds are quiet and receptive enough to receive what He has been waiting to communicate. Our task is to offer the Lord an open mind. Prayer is not seeking to convince the Lord of what we want, but the time of communion with Him in which He implants His thoughts in our minds. Our desires are transformed into His desires for us. He has created us to think clearly under the guidance of His indwelling Spirit in our thinking brain.

A Responsive Will

A responsive will is closely intertwined with an open mind. The will can be either an imperious sentinel guarding the door of a closed mind or a ready servant to carry out what the Lord articulates in our thoughts. The persistent prayer, "Lord make me willing to hear and desire what you want," is the key. Since He motivates the longing to pray that prayer, He is ready to answer it. The liberation of the will is one of the greatest aspects of God's healing Spirit we ever know. He does it by the power of love. Conditioned with the thought of His gracious care for us and repeated forgiveness of our failures, our wills become responsive to activating the guidance the Lord has given us. Then we can say with George Matheson:

My will is not my own
Till Thou hast made it Thine;
If I would reach a monarch's throne
It must its crown resign;

It only stands unbent
Amid the closing strife
When on Thy bosom it has leant
And found in Thee its life.[3]

A completely surrendered will opens the floodgate for
the Lord to work in our minds "to will and do His good
pleasure." We will not know His will or desire to do it until
we ask for the miraculous healing of our wills. We will
remain willful and stubborn until He sets us free.

A Faithful Obedience

Faithful obedience is the direct result of that freedom.
The Lord progressively reveals His will to those who act
on what He guides. Often we find it difficult to desire His
will in a crucial decision because we have resisted acting
on what He has clearly guided in other areas of our relationships and responsibilities. We get prepared for life's big
decisions by following through with obedience in what we
know He has asked us to do in daily faithfulness to Him.
We need to ask Him, "Lord, is there any area where I have
been unwilling? Give me courage to follow orders today so
that you can trust me with guidance in the future." We do
not know what demanding decisions are ahead. Preparation for them begins now.

I have found that journaling is a helpful discipline.
Keeping a daily journal of what action steps have become
clear in our prayers helps us remember what the Lord has
guided and what we have done about it. Each day as a part
of prayer and Bible study I try to log the insights I have
received and steps of obedience I feel the Lord guides. It
provides a good inventory when I return to my quiet time
the next day. I can check off things which have been done
and be reminded of unfinished orders. I also list specific

petitions for the Lord's will under each day's entry. It is a great source of gratitude and praise to go back over a year's record of requests for guidance and realize how the Lord answered. I am filled with thanksgiving for what He has done and refortified for the future.

A friend keeps me fortified with bound books containing blank sheets for my prayer journaling. In affirmation of my Scots heritage, the covers are tartan, closely resembling the Ogilvie clan tartan! Several are filled each year with the records of my daily prayer pilgrimage. But any notebook will do. The important thing is the autobiography of growth in the will of the Lord that I record. Each day we can record guidance received, steps to be taken, and decisions pending the direction the Lord will crystalize in our thoughts, implement through our wills, and accomplish through our actions. Prayer for the will of the Lord in our decisions becomes an exciting adventure.

Abraham Lincoln puts an exclamation point on what I've tried to communicate about the Lord's guidance in our decisions. During the dark days of the Civil War, the Lord gave him direction and strength. One hundred and twenty years ago, the same year he reestablished a National Day of Prayer, Lincoln said, "I have been driven many times to my knees by the overwhelming conviction that I had nowhere else to go; my own wisdom and that of all around me seemed insufficient for the day." And then, explaining the Lord's answers, the president said, "I have had so many evidences of His direction, so many instances of times when I have been controlled by some other power than my own will, that I cannot doubt that this power comes from God. I frequently see my way clear to a decision when I am conscious that I have not sufficient facts on which to found it. I am satisfied that, when the Almighty wants me to do, or not to do a particular thing, He finds a way of letting me know. I talk to God, and when I do, my mind seems relieved and a way is suggested."

Notes

1. William Barclay, Daily Study Bible. 1 John (Philadelphia, Westminster Press, 1959.
2. Paul Rees, from a sermon.
3. George Matheson, "Christ's Bondservant", James Dalton Morrison, ed., *Masterpieces of Religious Verse* (New York: Harper & Row Publisher, 1948), p. 757.

For Further Thought . . .

1. Are you in the midst of a life decision? What questions should you ask in determining whether or not the decision you are leaning toward is part of God's will?

2. What is God's ultimate will for every believer? Are you in God's ultimate will?

3. What gifts enable Christians to know God's will for us in every situation?

4. Keeping a daily journal of our prayers helps us remember how God has guided us to pray. Do you keep a daily journal of your prayers?

CHAPTER TEN

When You're Tempted to Give Up

There are two very different ways of saying, "I'm finished!" One is the triumphant expression of the delight of completion. The other is the discouraged admission of defeat. So often it is the latter. Life is littered with unfinished tasks, uncompleted goals, unfulfilled assignments, and unhealed relationships.

Living is like a race with many laps. Each lap is made up of tasks given us to do. In His providential management of life, the Lord gives each of us challenges which only we can do. And in our efforts to accomplish His assignment, we are often tempted to give up before we are finished.

We've all known times when we were tempted to give up on people, prospects, and demanding opportunities. Perhaps we are breathlessly running one of those laps right now. We are not sure we are going to make it. We need a second wind, or what joggers call the "runner's high" when suddenly new strength is given and we are able to exceed our natural capacities.

He Provides Perseverance

In this final chapter, I want to focus our attention on how the Lord gives us a very special gift for completing each lap of life's race. He gives it to us through the consistent communion of prayer. Thus far we've talked about what the Lord can do when we prayerfully entrust our needs to Him. Now we must claim what He does when He entrusts a task to us. He provides perseverance. It is a balanced blend of our persistence and His power. The winning combination is hard work and the acceptance of supernatural strength. The Lord can accomplish magnificent things through people who invest all that they have and are to do His will and depend on His rejuvenating replenishment. Perseverance is the difference between life's pressures finishing us and our finishing the task of each lap by God's grace and for His glory.

Think about the particular challenge of the lap you're running right now. You felt the urge to pray about a concern. You turned it over to the Lord. Then He gave it back to you with guidance for what you were to do according to His strategy and strength.

What is it for you? Perhaps it's some person in your life the Lord has called you to help. You've prayed prayers of intercession and the Lord has made you part of the answer by telling you what He wants you to be and do with that person. Or perhaps it is a project you feel called to tackle. Prayer has given you a vision of what needs to be done. You know you can't do it without the Lord's ever-present guidance and divine energy to follow through faithfully. Maybe it is in your church, or in some aching social problems in the community. You feel the burden to do something. Then the Lord shows you what He wants you to do.

We are all called to extend the kingdom, communicate love and grasp the opportunities the Lord gives us. Every Christian is responsible to be a contagious witness to individuals and to become involved in some area of society where people suffer or are debilitated by social injustice.

And in our churches we are to be cooperative, willing participants in the Lord's renaissance of the parish. He is on the move today, bringing churches back to basics and renewing them to be Spirit-empowered, Bible-centered laboratories of new life. There's a new wind blowing in the Church today. These are the most exciting days since the first century. When we pray about our congregations the Lord helps us to set goals only He could help us accomplish. Then He calls us to be partners with Him in reviving religious members who need a fresh experience of His power and in restructuring the Church to be a place where people can meet Him, grow as vital Christians, and become equipped to live out their faith in the tensions of the world.

It is after we've accepted our particular assignment and worked hard to accomplish it, that often we grow weary. Sometimes we face resistance which drains our enthusiasm. Things take longer than we expected. We become impatient with ourselves, others, even God. Discouragement sets in. We wish we could be free of the responsibility; resign from the Lord's assignment. We are tempted to give up!

The Lord Understands

The Lord understands. He's been dealing for centuries with people who feel they are finished before they finish. He is for us: He waits to give us exactly what we need to finish our present lap so we can get on to the next lap He's planned for us. He uses prayer not only to clarify our assignments but also as a channel for the flow of His perseverance each day. Prayer is not only for what the Lord does for us, but also for what He wants to do through us.

In order to claim how He gives perseverance I want to reintroduce you to one of the heroes of the Old Testament who was given an awesome task to do and show how he did it through the power of prayer. His life is a stirring example of perseverance—what it is and how we can receive it.

The patron saint of perseverance through prayer is Nehemiah. You may have anticipated that I would cite Moses, Job, or Elijah. But in my observation Nehemiah is a model for perseverance not only in difficulties, but in finishing what the Lord gave him to do. How he endured to the finish of a lap of the race of his life gives us a basis of drawing together the promises of God for perseverance.

In the year 445 B.C. Nehemiah was called to spearhead the rebuilding of the wall of Jerusalem. When the work was nearing completion and his enemies threatened his life, a false friend pleaded with him to come down off the wall being reconstructed and flee to a safe hiding place in the Temple. For Nehemiah that was tantamount to quitting when he was near reaching the goal the Lord had given him. What he said in response was to ask two questions and make a flat statement. "Should such a man as I flee? And who is there such as I who would go into the temple to save his life? I will not go in!" (Neh. 6:11). That could be the motto of those who refuse to give up and who receive perseverance from the Lord to finish.

A man such as I. What kind of person was Nehemiah? There are five things that occur to me as I study the book that bears his name. Each gives us a window to look into his character—and all in order provide us a progression for a perseverance profile.

Greatly Favored by God

First of all, Nehemiah was a person greatly favored by God. He was a second generation Hebrew in the Persian exile. By God's grace he had risen to a position of power

We can have determination to finish when we know we have been appointed and deployed by God to do a particular task.

as the cupbearer and advisor of King Artaxerxes in Shushan. But Nehemiah never forgot that he was a Hebrew and that his God was Yahweh. Through his growing years he was given training in the law and an exiled heart that had reverence for Jerusalem as the Holy City. The Lord guided his development as a man of strong character, faithfulness, and determination. One of the most crucial aspects of the Lord's favor is the healthy development of our wills. The balance between willingness and willfulness can be tipped so easily. The Lord wants us to grow as clear-thinking people guided by His Spirit with wills open to respond to His direction. His care for Nehemiah built a strong-willed man who could hear and obey Him and not falter under pressure.

Clearly Called

That leads us to the second aspect of his perseverance. Nehemiah was a person clearly called. We can have determination to finish when we know we have been appointed and deployed by God to do a particular task. His call began in a concern which grew into a conviction.

Some Hebrews from Judah told Nehemiah about conditions in the city of Jerusalem. The city had been destroyed in 586 B.C. when the Babylonians razed the city and carried off most of the population into exile. The Temple, the wall and the buildings of the city were left in rubble. In the spring of 458 B.C., through a decision of Artaxerxes, then the Persian emperor, Ezra led an expedition of Jews back to Jerusalem. They began reconstruction of the Temple and rebuilding of the wall. Then suddenly the work on the wall was stopped through conflict with the local Persian overlords. The report brought to Nehemiah was that the despicable condition of the city was matched by the dejected spirit of the Jews who were living in worse circumstances than they had known in exile. When Nehemiah heard this sad news, he felt a warrant in his soul to rebuild the walls of Jerusalem.

He fasted and prayed. His prayer was one of praise and the specific petition that he would be given favor in the king's sight. Nehemiah knew that only the Lord could move the heart of the king to release him. And the Lord was faithful. When He gives us an assignment, He clears the way for us to do His will.

The Lord answered Nehemiah's prayer in an astounding way. When the cupbearer and advisor to the king appeared to serve him, his face was downcast. The king inquired about the cause of this uncustomary sadness in the Hebrew. Nehemiah relayed the burden on his troubled heart. "Why should my face not be sad, when the city, the place of my fathers' tombs, lies waste, and its gates are burned with fire?" (2:3). The king asked a crucial question, "What do you want me to do?" Before Nehemiah answered he prayed and then asked to be sent to Judah to rebuild Jerusalem. The Lord was guiding each step of the conversation. The response of the king was not only to give Nehemiah permission to go but he willingly granted his request for letters from the king for safe travel from Persia to Judah and for cooperation from the local leaders over the area. He would need timber from the king's forest to make beams for the gates, but most of all he would need the king's blessing and authority as leverage with the leaders who would probably resist any rise of the Jews to patriotism and power. All that Nehemiah asked was granted by Artaxerxes and he set off for Jerusalem. The Hebrew was clearly called and the Lord who called him confirmed His guidance in the miraculous opening of Artaxerxes' mind and his willingness to affirm his servant's mission.

Richly Blessed

Third, we see Nehemiah as a person richly blessed. The Lord had equipped him through the years with great leadership ability and the impelling gifts of a leader. He had charisma, the capacity to impart a vision, the skill to organize people, and the enthusiasm to work with them until the task was finished.

When he arrived in Jerusalem he saw the walls in shambles and felt the depleted hope of his people. The Lord not only wanted Nehemiah to rebuild the walls but to reconstruct a new confidence and self-esteem in His discouraged people. With Spirit-birthed urgency in his voice, Nehemiah rallied the people. "You see the distress that we are in, how Jerusalem lies waste, and its gates are burned with fire. Come let us build the walls of Jerusalem, that we may no longer be a reproach" (2:17). He told the people that the call to do that had come from God. Their response was inspired by His Spirit. "Let us rise up and build" (v. 18). The Lord gives a vision and then gives us people who are ignited with the same vision in order to help us accomplish our assigned task.

But great work for the Lord is seldom done without opposition from both enemies and friends. Nehemiah had both. How he dealt with that reveals him as a person who consistently prayed and was repeatedly strengthened. We see a man who faced impossible odds with the perseverance received in prayer.

Nehemiah's enemies were the local Persian overlords who saw him as a threat to their positions. These were joined by the Samaritan leaders. They feared the rising unity and vigilance of the Jews. When they observed Nehemiah's charisma for leadership and saw the response of the people to rebuilding the wall, first they laughed with scorn and then were gripped by hatred. Their power was being threatened. A power struggle is usually behind most negative criticism and eventually turns it into open hostility.

In spite of the opposition, Nehemiah marshalled the Jews to action and the work of reconstruction of the walls began. He divided the wall and its gates into sections and assigned the various parts to families in Jerusalem and teams of Jews from nearby cities. The work proceeded with perseverance inspired by the leader's prayers for strength.

Every means was used by the hostile enemies to debilitate Nehemiah's determination. Rumor, intrigue, and finally, organized armed attacks made the work of rebuilding perilous.

The progress was further crippled by dissension among some of the Jews whose equivocation was threatened by Nehemiah's courage and determination. We all know what that means. Sometimes our most difficult antagonists are the very people we are trying to help. Few things contribute more to our temptation to give up than that. We border on saying, "What's the use? The very people the Lord has asked me to help don't want Him or the task He's given us to do together." I hear that from discouraged church leaders often when they take themselves too seriously and don't take their need for moment-by-moment replenishment of His strength seriously enough. And yet, if we ask the Lord for fresh perseverance, He provides it. He is more concerned about our finishing the lap than we may be! He doesn't give up and doesn't give us the luxury of giving in to people's attitudes. As leaders we can accomplish God's assignments only when we draw security from Him, and not those He's given us to lead. Nehemiah had that single-minded determination. "The God of heaven Himself will prosper us;

therefore we His servants will arise and build" (v. 20).
And rise up and build is what they did. The reason was a
dynamic mixture of trust in God and loyalty to Nehemiah.

A Man Greatly Admired

The fourth thing we observe about the dynamic leader
is that he was a man greatly admired. The people trusted
him because of his prayer-saturated vision that they could
finish the rebuilding. People long to rise to the finest we
dare to picture they can be. When we communicate that
we are for them and not against them, they will give their
utmost. That also requires working with them in the
accomplishment of the dream. Nehemiah did not adminis-
trate the rebuilding from an aloof director's office, sending
out impersonal memos of what he wanted done. He was
there on the wall laboring night and day with his fellow
Jews. Certainly, Nehemiah directed the work and
depended on the follow-through of others. But all the people could see and feel the impact of his indefatigable commitment to finish the task by giving the people himself as
well as his vision. That's why he could not flee and take
refuge in the Temple.

When the rebuilding was nearing completion, Nehemiah's enemies conspired together and threatened to raise
up an army to stop the work. He devised a plan for half of
the Jews to stand guard while the other half held spears to
protect them. In addition each worker held his own sword
and trumpeters were stationed to sound the alarm in case
of attack. Nehemiah's watchword was, "Our God will fight
for us" (4:20).

When threats of attack did not dissuade Nehemiah and
the builders, other tactics were devised. The enemies of
the leader tried to distract him with conferences to talk.
They tried to get his attention with false accusations that

he and the Jews planned to rebel and that he was grooming himself to be king of Judea. He flatly denied the charge and refused to stop work for disputations with them. Prayer was Nehemiah's secret weapon. And what did he pray for in the pressure? Perseverance. Listen to the courage in his voice when he responds to the challenge to stop the work to consult with his enemies. "I am doing a great work, so that I cannot come down. Why should the work cease while I leave it and go down to you?" (6:3). That courage came from the quality of Nehemiah's prayers. "But now, O God, strengthen my hands."

That led his enemies to try one further method of discrediting the great leader. He went to visit one of the Jews who was confined to his home. Again we see Nehemiah's personal care for individuals. The man's name was Shemaiah. What Nehemiah did not know was that the man was an informer. Strange twist. The man had pretended sickness to get Nehemiah to visit him so he could plead with him to flee from the wall and find safety in the Temple. The plot was to expose him as one who was frightened. Shemaiah's plea was drenched with factious concern for Nehemiah. "Let us meet together in the house of God, within the temple, and let us close the doors of the temple, for they are coming to kill you . . . at night" (6:10). Nehemiah's response to this beguiling concern for his welfare reveals the fifth and final thing I want to underline about his perseverance. He was a person courageously unafraid. That enabled him to make the statement we quoted earlier which has given courage to so many who have noted it in tight places through the centuries. "Should such a man as I flee? Who is there, that, being such as I would go into the temple to save his life? I will not go in" (Neh. 6:11, ASV).

Feared No One

Nehemiah feared no person. His relationship with the Lord through prayer gave him the freedom to want to please Him and not people. People-pleasers will always be afraid. They are taking their signals from the wrong source. Repeatedly in the Old Testament we are admonished to fear the Lord. The Hebrew word means "awe and wonder." That quality of reverence is the antidote to our fears. It produces daring and boldness. When our only concern is to know and do the Lord's will, we need be afraid of no person or group.

Note that Nehemiah did not think of the Temple or worship as an escape from danger. So often we think of getting out of difficulties into the comfort of prayer. That's not authentic prayer. Prayer gives us the fearlessness to stay in the battle. Dr. Alexis Carrell in *Man, the Unknown* said, "Prayer is the most powerful form of energy that one can generate. In prayer we link ourselves with the inexhaustible power that spins the universe. Prayer is a force as real as terrestrial gravity. The influence of prayer on the human mind and body is as demonstrable as that of secreting glands. Its results can be measured in terms of increased physical buoyancy, greater intellectual vigor, moral stamina, and a deeper understanding of the realities underlying human relationships. Only in prayer do we achieve that complete and harmonious assembly of body, mind, and spirit which gives the frail human reed its unshakable strength."[1]

That's what prayer did for Nehemiah and can do for us when we are tempted to give up. In prayer we give in to the inflow of the Lord's power so that we do not need to give up to the desire to be safe. Prayer is not a retreat

People of unshakable vision and indefatigable perseverance are those who have been with the Lord long enough, consistently enough, and deeply enough to know that He delights to help us accomplish the impossible dreams He gives us.

from danger; it is the secret source of courage to finish. People of unshakable vision and indefatigable perseverance are those who have been with the Lord long enough, consistently enough, and deeply enough to know that He delights to help us accomplish the impossible dreams He gives us.

Nehemiah finished the building of the wall to the glory of God. The Jews were amazed and their enemies were discouraged. Here are Nehemiah's own words of triumph. "So the wall was finished on the twenty-fifth day of the month of Elul, in fifty-two days. And it happened, when all our enemies heard of it, and all the nations around us saw these things, that they were very disheartened in their own eyes; for they perceived that this work was done by our God" (6:15-16). There is no limit to the perseverance the Lord will give when we are willing to give Him the glory. He is pleased to astound the people around us with the resiliency and resoluteness He gives to those who refuse to give up.

The greatest temptation had come to Nehemiah to flee and not finish the work when he was close to completion. That often happens. Our exhaustion is most excruciating as we are nearing the end of the lap. That's when we need an inflow of supernatural power. The Lord says, "Don't give up. I am with you. Press on. Victory is within your grasp!"

It is in prayer that we put our roots down deeply into the limitless reservoir of God's strength. When we tell the Lord we are tempted to give up, that we are dangerously close to being engulfed with our problems, then He gives us the stamina to keep on steadfastly.

A clergy friend of mine was tempted to quit. He was drained and depleted. In despair, he went to a spiritually sensitive older friend. She empathized, and then put her finger on the raw nerve. "You are like a pump unconnected to a well. People have pumped you dry. Your greatest need is to reestablish contact with the Lord. People need Him, not your knowledge, adequacy or cleverness. Instead of quitting, take a week off for silence with the Lord. Allow Him to heal your hurts and meet your needs. Stop working for the Lord and let Him work through you."

The man was stunned by the woman's directness. The Lord was at work and gave him the honesty to accept the piercing advice. He secured a retired pastor to fill his pulpit the following Sunday and went into the mountains for a full-week retreat of silence. Exhausted in body and soul, he slept for the first full day and night. Then he began to allow the Lord to refocus his life's purpose and goals. That was followed with long walks in which he asked the Lord to show him what He wanted him to do to complete the lap of his life in the parish he was serving. Most of all, he allowed the Lord to meet his own needs for replenishment. He returned to work a new man. With his priorities redefined, he reestablished his own time of daily prayer and meditation which had previously been edged out by busy-ness. The greatest gift he could give his congregation was to do more than say his prayers; to spend prolonged time in prayer. He began living in the stream of the Lord's power. The result was that he now had an indefatigable supply of inspiration and wisdom as well as joy and hope to give to his people. He is finishing the lap of renewing his present parish. After that the Lord will have another lap for him to run. He told me that his fondest hope is that he will never forget what he's discovered in this lap of the race.

Winston Churchill said in dark days when his countrymen were tempted to become discouraged, "Never give in! Never give in! Never, never, never—in anything great or small, large or petty—never give in except to convictions of honor and good sense." To take and apply that admonition we need more than human pertinacity; we need God-given perseverance.

James reminds us that faith without works is dead. So too, prayer without work is ineffective. But equally so, work without consistent prayer will wear us out. The Lord never assigns us more to do than we can accomplish with His replenishing power. He guides the task, gives the strength to do it, and keeps us going until we finish. Don't give up!

We are back to where we started our journey together in search of the secret of praying with power. Prayer starts with God. He is the initiator of the challenges of each lap of the race of life. And He never gives up on us regardless of our failures and weakness. With that assurance we can ask Nehemiah's question. "Can a person like me flee?" No! What the Lord did for Nehemiah through prayer, He will do for us and so much more. We live on this side of Calvary. Christ endured the cross for our forgiveness. When He completed the atonement for us, He cried, "It is finished!" Because of that we never need say in despair, "I'm finished!" We are never finished sharing the love and hope we have in Christ and working in His strength to accomplish each lap of the race. In a way, our confidence of eternal life enables us to run each lap with the assurance that we've already won the race!

Note

1. Dr. Alexis Carrell, *Man, the Unknown* (New York: Hillman-Mac-Fadden, 1961).

For Further Thought . . .

1. What specific gift does God give all believers for completing "each lap of life's race"?

2. How did our Old Testament hero Nehemiah exhibit perseverance? Is there a task or goal you are working on that you have been tempted to give up and "flee"? Have you called upon God's gift of perseverance?

3. When God gives us an assignment, He also gives us a promise. What is that promise? Will He ever give us more than we can accomplish with His replenishing power? What should we do when we are tempted to give up?

4. Every believer will be called to complete specific works throughout his Christian life. But there is one task we are all called to that we will never finish. What is that task?

ENRICH YOUR LIFE WITH THESE CHALLENGING REGAL BOOKS

Unleashing Your Potential: Discovering Your God-Given Opportunities for Ministry   Frank R. Tillapaugh
The author decries the fortress mentality that prevents too many churches from engaging in much needed ministries beyond their walls. He calls every Christian to serve and challenges every church to reach outside itself.   5418972

God's Transforming Love: Daily Reflections on His Life-Changing Power
Lloyd John Ogilvie
This book contains the very best of Lloyd John Ogilvie's writings thematically compiled. Each selection can be read in a few minutes and will leave you inspired and invigorated in heart and mind.   5111794

A Moment a Day: Practical Devotions for Today's Busy Woman
Compiled by Mary Beckwith and Kathi Mills
Over 100 special devotions by leading Christian women written for women in all walks of life. These short devotions show how God is at work in your family, your friendships, and your day-to-day life. Contributors include Shirley Dobson, Jill Briscoe, Gloria Gaither and many others.   5419516

Won by One: Helping Your Friends and Those Closest to You Enjoy a Relationship with Jesus Christ   Ron Rand
The author presents a variety of ways in which Christians can simply, winsomely, sensitively and effectively use personal relationships to win friends and relatives to Jesus Christ.   5419235

Yet Will I Trust Him: Accepting the Sovereignty of God in Times of Need
Peg Rankin
The return of a classic Bible study on accepting God's will in all areas of our lives.   5419458

The Journey of a Disciple: The Christian's Pilgrimage from Decision to Discipleship   Stuart and Jill Briscoe
Join the Briscoes as they walk in the footsteps of the first disciples through Corinth, Philippi, Athens, Jerusalem and other cities and learn the complete commitment that Christ asks from His followers. Leader's Guide and video series also available.   5419145

LOOK FOR THESE AND OTHER EXCITING REGAL TITLES AT YOUR REGULAR CHRISTIAN BOOKSTORE OR CALL
1-800-235-3415 (outside CA) OR 1-800-227-4025 (inside CA)